Writing for Readers

Lucy Calkins and Natalie Louis

Photography by Peter Cunningham

HEINEMANN ◆ PORTSMOUTH, NH

This book is dedicated to Jimmy, with gigantic, humongous thanks for making it all possible.

Heinemann
361 Hanover Street
Portsmouth, NH 03801–3912
www.heinemann.com

Offices and agents throughout the world

Cataloging-in-Publication data is on file with the Library of Congress.

ISBN-13: 978-0-325-04721-8

Production: Elizabeth Valway, David Stirling, and Abigail Heim
Cover and interior designs: Jenny Jensen Greenleaf
Series includes photographs by Peter Cunningham, Nadine Baldasare, and Elizabeth Dunford
Composition: Publishers' Design and Production Services, Inc.
Manufacturing: Steve Bernier

Printed in the United States of America on acid-free paper
20 19 18 17 16 VP 10 9 8 7 6

Acknowledgments

ONCE YOU ARE ALL GROWN-UP, there aren't that many times in life when you get to stand and toast the people who make it all possible. Weddings, graduations, and sometimes birthdays, if there's a big party. Given the amount of gratitude we feel, this is an occasion when thank-yous seem especially important.

So the two of us really love this page. It is our chance to say it loud and clear: all that we are, all that we do, all that we imagine is only possible because of the support and education that we receive from an amazing group of people. There aren't many footnotes in this book—one doesn't usually footnote the little pep talks one gives to five-year-olds—but every page is laden with fingerprints of others who have made this teaching what it is.

First, the two of us are grateful to each other. We've been friends, colleagues, coconspirators, writing partners, and learning partners for more than 15 years. Our ideas are intertwined, and welded together by our voices, experiences, and knowledge.

Then we are grateful to the Teachers College Reading and Writing Project as an organization that has sustained us and given us an intellectual home. The people who are officially on the staff of the TCRWP have changed some over the years, but the community, by and large, grows only larger as the network grows. We're particularly grateful to Amanda Hartman, Kathleen Tolan, and Laurie Pessah, who help make our work possible.

It may look at first glance that this is a book about writing, but it is also a book about reading and about phonics, too, and the thinking bears the imprint of so many colleagues who have nurtured our thinking in those areas. We are especially grateful to the late Marie Clay, founder of Reading Recovery, who came to the TCRWP annually, often visiting classrooms with us, and deepened our thinking in ways too big to name. We are also grateful to Donald Bear, and to Irene Fountas and Gay Su Pinnell for informing our work. Mary Ann Colbert has always pushed us to think about and to ever deepen our understanding of the beginning reading process.

The seed idea for this book was germinated in a think tank of teacher leaders in 2001–2002, and we are thankful to all the members of that group. Abby Smith (coauthor of *Small Moments*) and Pat Bleichman were especially important to the thinking in this book, and some of Pat and Lucy's book *The Craft of Revision* from the original Units of Study for Primary Writing series informs the last bend of this book. And we were deeply influenced that school year by the teaching, knowledge, and passion of Joanna Uhry from Fordham University.

Many others have added their knowledge and wisdom to the book: Kate Montgomery talked us through the very sticky melding of revision and editing. Special thanks go to our longtime friend Zoë Ryder White, a pro at teaching kindergartners and bringing their quirky ways to the page. Teva Blair always seemed to provide or send just the right editorial help. We also want to thank Kerry Herlihy and Abby Heim for chasing down the important details and never losing the thread.

To all those we have named, and to all we could have named, a special kindergarten toast.

The class described in this unit is a composite class, with children and partnerships of children gleaned from classrooms in very different contexts, then put together here. We wrote the units this way to bring you both a wide array of wonderful, quirky, various children and also to illustrate for you the predictable (and unpredictable) situations and responses this unit has created in classrooms across the nation and world.

—Natalie and Lucy

Contents

Bend III   Partnering for Revision: Making Stories More Fun to Read

Bend IV   Preparing for Publication

Welcome to the Unit

KINDERGARTEN CHILDREN TELL THE TRUTH. "Boring," they call out if your lesson is too long. Or "What's that red spot on your nose?" In this unit, you have the perfect opportunity to draw on this natural instinct of your youngsters as you channel them to tell true stories from their lives. You will also invite your students to face a new truth, one they won't have heard before now: writing a successful story requires that they put enough letters into words that their readers can decipher what they are trying to say. In short, then, this unit teaches children strategies for making clearer, richer stories and helps them strengthen the conventions and mechanics of their writing.

If now seems early in the year to address your students' abilities to communicate clearly and conventionally, know that the unit has been piloted with thousands of kindergarten classrooms in a diverse range of schools and has been a great hit. But yes, it is certainly the case that some kindergartners will be more poised at this time of year than others to actually succeed at writing readable texts. We've tried to keep that in mind while writing this and have found that inviting kids to engage in the work of trying to hear and record sounds, of getting help from others and from name charts and alphabet charts, is good work for kids who don't come to kindergarten knowing their alphabet. But we are also aware that some of you will feel that instead of teaching this as your second unit in the year, you'll want to rely on the resources in the *If . . . Then . . . Curriculum* book to teach another unit prior to this one, giving children a bit more time to grow into this challenging work. Our general feeling is that before you teach this unit, you'll want to make sure that your children see writing as a way to make and communicate meaning, to share their own important stories. They must be able to generate ideas for writing and to write (or tell) stories that stretch across several pages. Ideally, we hope that children enter this unit as fearless (if not skilled!) spellers. That is, you hope that the child who wants to write about a bulldozer will have the courage and confidence to tackle the word *bulldozer* even if he hears only a very few sounds. If your children enter this unit driven by a desire to tell their stories, then they won't sacrifice their wonderful content when you nudge them to write more conventionally.

The unit is aligned with the expectations for kindergartners laid out by the Common Core State Standards. Specifically, this unit sets children up to address the Standards for Writing, which channel kindergartners to "use a combination of drawing, dictating, and writing to narrate a single event or several loosely linked events, tell about the events in the order in which they occurred, and provide a reaction to what happened" (W K.3), and with the Standards for Language, which expect students to "demonstrate a command of standard English grammar and usage when speaking or writing," as well as "capitalization, punctuation, and spelling when writing" (L K.1, K.2). This unit also begins to set children up for success with some of the first-grade Common Core standards.

This unit grows out of two books from the original Units of Study for Primary Writing series, the original *Writing for Readers* and *The Craft of Revision*, coauthored with Pat Bleichman. We've kept the best that each of those books had to offer, brought in all our newest knowledge of methods for teaching writing, raised the level of teaching so that the book would address both the Common Core and Webb's Depth of Knowledge, and drawn on the last decade of work in schools.

For those of you who are familiar with the original K–2 units of study, one thing you will notice right away is that the focus of this book is not on *small moment* writing, but on *true story* writing. We have found that while some kindergarten children are ready to write tightly focused stories, others are not. So, for now, a child might write, "I rode my bike. I got ice cream. I went home." And you will want to embrace that as a terrific true story. There are lots of ways to make the story better, but we found that previously, our methods steered many kindergarten teachers to respond invariably to a story such as that by calling for the young author to zoom in to a more tightly focused tale. That is one reasonable way to lift the level of the story, but there are a lot of other possibilities as well, and we felt that in kindergarten, it is premature for teachers and children to be hypervigilant about a story's focus. For now, the important thing is for children to become accustomed to thinking of a story, capturing it in drawings and words that span pages, and doing all this in ways that they, and others, can read.

One big goal of the unit, then, is to help children put actual words and sentences onto the page. You'll teach them to sound out words, stretching the words out so they can isolate and hear the sounds at the start of a word, and to make marks to represent those sounds. You'll teach them how to mark the end of a sentence and when to do so with a period or a question mark or an exclamation point.

Of course, if children are going to approach spelling and punctuation with the same resourcefulness, verve, and energy that they bring to the rest of the writing curriculum, we must approach the teaching of conventions with equal resourcefulness, verve, and energy. Therefore, you'll want to make word walls, blends, and capital letters into the talk of the town. We know, of course, that it will take far more than a single unit of study for children to grow strong in their abilities to write conventionally, but we also know that there can be great benefits to shining a curricular spotlight on the critical importance of conventions.

It will be important that children can reread the books they write, turning the pages from front to back, reading them from left to right, top to bottom. They will continue to work in partnerships, as they did during the first unit, sharing their booklets just as reading workshop partners share their books. Partnership work supports the Common Core's expectation that kindergartners engage in "collaborative conversations," with multiple exchanges in which they "speak audibly and express their thoughts, feelings, and ideas clearly" (SL K.1, K.6). In partnerships, you'll want children to read in two ways: telling the story using rich, oral storytelling language and then reading the print, touching the words as they read them. They can sit hip-to-hip, hold

the booklet between them, turn pages (ideally from left to right), and tell the story as they study the pictures and read the writing. They can begin working on one-to-one matching as they name the things that they see on the page and read the labels under each of those items. By the end of the month, if not before, some of your children will have graduated from writing labels alone to writing a sentence underneath the picture they have drawn on each page. Those sentences will be structured into stories.

While this is a writing unit, it also teaches and invites students to practice some of the reading foundational skills (CCSS K.RFS.1, 2 and 3). This is just as it should be. Of the four literacy processes, writing is the slowest, and so writing workshop is the perfect place to teach children how to break words into their component sounds and then to match symbols to those sounds. Writing is a big reason to learn these foundational skills in the first place. When you have something to say on paper, you need the skills to get the symbols on the page to help you do your talking.

Of course, to a large degree, you'll let your students determine how the unit will go. That is, their particular strengths and needs as writers will factor into your instructional decisions.

OVERVIEW OF THE UNIT

Until now, you've so wanted your children to feel good as writers that you have hidden your struggles to translate their spindly letters into meaning. In fact, you've no doubt reveled in children's approximations. When neither you nor the child could decipher a text, you have tended to distract the child from this state of affairs by turning quickly to the picture or to the next story—anything to avoid this child confronting the sad fact that, alas, the work of his hands isn't readable. The problem with this is that the only reason children will care about spelling, punctuation, or white space is that these conventions make it easier for others to read and to appreciate their texts! It's crucial, therefore, that as soon as children have the ability to begin to write in ways a reader could conceivably read, you let them in on the truth.

This unit of study begins, then, with you confessing to your children that you have a hard time reading their writing. "I took your wonderful stories home last night," you'll say, "and I sat down to read them. But do you know what? I couldn't figure out what the story was supposed to say! Has that ever happened to any of you?" You'll quickly follow this up with an invitation to children to review their stories as readers, deciding which are clear and which need work still. Children will make two piles: easy-to-read writing and hard-to-read writing. These piles can serve as data for you; as you review them, you will discover ways to tailor the lessons in this first bend to meet the individualized needs of your students.

Right away, then, you'll challenge your writers not only to tell the true stories of their lives, but to do so through writing that is easy for others to read. Early in this bend, you'll encourage children to draw on all that they know about writing stories, steering them to review an old anchor chart on writing true stories. As children work, you will address the print on the page and encourage your writers to write words in more conventional ways. In the spirit of audience, this bend of the unit also includes a session on using drawing to plan and rehearse more meaningful stories and more exact storytelling language. The bend ends with you teaching children two crucial skills to make their writing more clear: writing in sentences and rereading their work as they write.

In Bend II, you'll give your students additional tools and opportunities to make their writing more powerful and even clearer for their readers. You'll begin by teaching children how to use a checklist to reflect on what they have learned so far this year. The next two sessions are designed to strengthen your students' word-writing skills by spotlighting the use of vowels and sight words. As soon as you teach kids how to write words better, you will find that some children will need the next session in this bend to balance their focus. As a result, you will probably want to teach your children to listen for and capture their true storytelling words, not just the easier-to-spell words. In the next few sessions, you will teach your writers the power of partnerships as they aim to make their writing clearer. The bend ends with a session that challenges children to use everything they have learned to make writing that is easy for readers to read.

In Bend III, the focus shifts from getting readable words on the page to telling stories more powerfully through the use of revision. Again, you'll talk up the power of working in partnerships to support this work. This bend begins and ends with attention to the whole story. In the first session, you'll teach your writers how to mine their drawings to find more story to tell. The middle of this bend teaches your children how to use flaps to make additions to stories. This very concrete work of adding writing real estate to a booklet makes flaps one of the most attractive tools for little kids learning about the power of revision. The final lesson sets children up to work as peer partners to help each other make their stories clearer and easier to read.

In the final bend, students learn the process of taking a single piece of writing to publication. You'll challenge your kids to select a piece they will share at the end of the unit and to use all they have learned to make the piece shine. Since this entire unit has highlighted both the editing and revision stages of the writing process, your children will do both on the first day. Then, children will work on creating more satisfying endings, ones that introduce a big feeling. Next, you'll help your writers make their pieces beautiful and ready for a larger audience. The final celebration of this unit is making a product, perhaps a bulletin board or a celebration in which children read their work out loud to an audience. It is also an opportunity for writers to self-assess the work they have done.

ASSESSMENT

Before you launch this second unit, make sure that you have conducted an on-demand assessment of your children in narrative writing. (Hopefully, you did such an assessment at the start of the year, in which case it is up to you whether you want to do another one now.) Specific instructions to offer children are included in *Writing Pathways: Performance Assessments and Learning Progressions, K–5*.

At the end of this unit and before turning to another type of writing altogether, do another assessment so that you and your children can see the growth they will have made through Units 1 and 2. You'll be able to say to your kids, "Look at what you did earlier in the year. And oh, my goodness, *now*, look what you can do!" And this won't be hyperbole; their leaps in growth will be evident on the page. The good news is that these assessments will also offer you a means to measure the effectiveness of your teaching and to determine next steps for whole-class, small-group, and one-on-one instruction.

It is especially important that you and your grade level colleagues administer and assess the writing tasks under similar conditions and with similar understandings so that you can compare results. We recommend that whoever decides to alter the task in any way, that decision be discussed beforehand with his or her team so that everyone agrees to the same conditions.

As children are drawing and writing on their on-demand assessments, move quickly among them, asking them to tell you what they are writing and then recording verbatim what they say, as a dictation. Usually teachers record each youngster's intended message on a Post-it® that they later stick onto the back of the writing. Later, when you collect students' writing and try to understand whether their spelling was somewhat phonetic, for example, you'll find that the record of what the writer intended to say will help you decipher what she wrote and what the logic was that informed her writing. The dictation of the writing also helps you understand the differences between the oral language abilities and the word-writing abilities of your students.

As you conduct conferences and lead small groups, remember to gather data that will inform your teaching of the whole class, small groups and individuals. Use your conferring notes to record and recall this data during the unit. Be careful not to ask your kindergartners tons of questions about their writing process. Instead of asking them to talk all about their process, angle your work toward helping them actually do the work they need to do and to understand why. You will also want to establish some sort of routine for looking through every child's writing folder at least once every week. As you do this, it is helpful to again choose a lens, a way of looking at the work. Both your conferring notes and your observations of children's folders can serve as a formative assessment to guide your teaching decisions.

As you look across the work that students do at the start of this unit, and in the middle of the unit, you should see dramatic and obvious improvements in their spelling and their control of the conventions of written language. A child who starts the unit writing right to left, bottom to top, will end the unit writing left to right, top to bottom, and adding punctuation to boot! A child who begins with no letter-sound connection can, within a matter of weeks, be using a dozen letters and sounds. As you support your kindergartners in this work, they will demonstrate an understanding of the organization and features of print, transferring their knowledge of reading texts to writing texts (CCSS RF K.1).

As in all writing units, the growth that individual students make will look different. If you have ELLs who are in the first two stages of language acquisition, before children produce English, you will want to tell them what you see on their pages as a way of supporting their language development. You might place your finger on a part of their drawing and observe, "Look at your writing! Is this you?" The child can respond with a "yes" or a "no." Then you can ask, "Are you in the park?" If the child nods, continue your observation and pointing, saying, "I see a tree. I see the sun. Look at all the flowers!" This

way, the child will have meaningful language experience between the teacher, the words, and her own drawings. Additionally, this process can be a kind of scaffold for students who are reluctant to talk about their writing. Keep in mind that the guidance you offer students will, of course, look different as you move from one to another during your one-to-one conferring and small-group instruction.

Another big goal in this unit will be for your writers to generate true, sequenced, cohesive stories from their lives and then record these stories across the pages of little booklets. Teach your students to use drawings to help them hold onto meaning and to help them generate the language of their stories. Teach them to label several items on each page and that sometimes labels consist of multiple words.

GETTING READY

Some children will come to school with a strong background in storytelling, while others will have close to none. Literacy scholar Shirley Brice Heath says the most important thing an adult can do to support a child's literacy is to immerse the child in a culture of storytelling. Parents are naturals at scaffolding children to re-create events. For instance, a child and her dad return from the park, and the mother says, "What did you do at the park?" The child says, "I swinged," and the mother replies, "Did you?! Did Daddy push you on the swings?" The child nods and says, "Daddy pushed me and I go high. I touched the tree." The mother nods, and retells the story. "Wow. Daddy pushed you on the swing! You went so high that you touched the leaves of the tree." This re-creation of the story is essential to learning how a sentence in standard English should go, and it supports the Language Standards of the Common Core, which expect kindergartners to begin using standard English grammar when writing or speaking (K.1). This oral storytelling not only pushes kids toward such command of grammar when speaking, but it also supports their ability to write stories in a clear and cohesive way.

The Common Core State Standards in Writing expect kindergartners to use a combination of drawing, dictating and writing to narrate a single event (K.3). Because children need to learn to talk a genre before they can write a genre, you will want to find ways to get children to tell each other stories from their lives. As part of this, we suggest you help them recall events the class has experienced together and then spin those events into stories (oral accounts).

The events can be small ones, for example, about the little inchworm that crawled across the page of the book during shared reading or the fire drill, during which the whole class went outside with the rest of the school. Say, "I love to think back and remember special moments like that, don't you? Let's all do that together. What happened first? Who can get us started by telling us just the first thing that happened? Then what? Who can tell us what happened next?" That is, you will show your little writers that people take the events of their lives and shape them into stories. On one day, you might teach students that you can zoom in on the important parts of what happened and tell the story of just that event. On another day, you might show students that you actually wrote the story you'd told the previous day onto paper, and that now you, like the children, can reread your own story. In this manner, you will create a few stories that the class knows well, and you will refer to those mentor texts often when children write. You might, for example, refer to one such text to point out that writers put a period at the end of a sentence, and you might also refer to it to point out that you told what happened first, then next and next, suggesting children do likewise. Of course, the important thing is not that you are telling and writing stories, but that the children are doing so—and doing so at a great clip.

Another way to practice this rich storytelling work is to have children bring in objects from home that hold meaning and to then tell the stories of those items. You might think of this as show-and-tell, and it is not altogether different—just imagine twenty-five children all showing and telling simultaneously, each to his or her partner! Some teachers have found it helpful and fun to have separate storytelling time. If children story-tell at the start of the day or after recess, becoming accustomed to spinning the events of their lives into sequential tales, then during writing workshop it will be especially easy for them to think of stories they can capture on the page. On some days, you will set children up to story-tell to a partner at the start of writing time, using this as an early form of rehearsal for narrative writing. Eventually, writers will be able to do this out-loud storytelling by themselves in whisper voices or in their heads.

For children to write stories, they'll need to hear stories read aloud. A deep immersion in the sounds of stories will help children as they now try to write the episodes of their lives as stories. Remind them that what they are doing during writing time is writing stories just like those they are reading during reading time. The only difference is that their stories, for now, are true ones. It will help if you read some stories that resemble the personal narratives your children will be writing. *Shortcut* by Donald Crews, *A Day with Daddy* by Nikki Grimes, and *The Snowy Day* by Ezra Jack Keats are all personal narratives that could serve as mentor texts, but be sure to use some of your personal favorites as well. Ideally, outside the writing workshop, throughout the school day, you will have found many opportunities to read and reread stories to children. If you are following our organization's (The Teachers College Reading and Writing Project's) curricular calendar for reading, for example, your students will be coming to know some stories so well that they can approximate reading these, turning the pages of a story like *Caps for Sale* by Esphyr Slobodkina.

Writing for Readers

IN THIS SESSION, you'll teach students that writers reread their writing to make sure that it is easy to read. If it is not, they go back and fix it up so that others can read it.

GETTING READY

- ✓ Student writing folders, filled with writing from the past unit, laid out like a seating chart in the meeting area (see Connection)

- ✓ Invented-spelling story on a chart paper booklet with the first two pages readable and the final page indecipherable—make it a cliffhanger (see Connection)

- ✓ Chart paper holding a page of enlarged student writing (see Teaching)

- ✓ Chart paper, marker (see Mid-Workshop Teaching)

- ✓ Sample of student writing where the student reread and then fixed up the writing to make it more readable, enlarged on chart paper (see Share)

- ✓ Supply of stapled-together blank story booklets of three to four pieces of paper as at the end of the previous unit. Renew the supply every day.

- ✓ Children in partnerships. These partnerships should be carried over from the previous unit.

COMMON CORE STATE STANDARDS: W.K.3, RFS.K.1, RFS.K.2, RFS.K.3, SL.K.1, L.K.1, L.K.2

D URING THIS UNIT, a good deal of your teaching will aim to help children write more conventionally. The unit, however, continues to channel children to pay attention to content, craft, and process while it also supports a new awareness of conventions. It is a big challenge for writers to expand the number of things they are working on to include an attention to conventions while they are still striving to tell and write focused, lively true stories, but that is the work of the unit.

Remember, children will have just begun writing personal narratives. Especially because they are new to that work, there is a lot of room for growth! Simply providing them with time to tell and write stories to each other and opportunities to mess about with story language and structure will be important. Through an immersion in stories, they'll come to internalize the fact that in stories, one thing happens and then the next and the next. Across the first few months of kindergarten, children's stories can develop in ways that are truly astonishing. During this unit, your youngsters will become more adept and independent in choosing topics for their true stories, storytelling those stories, touching-and-telling the pages, and working to make lively, detailed, well-structured little narratives.

But the unit begins in this session with a new element—a focus on writing stories in such a way that another person can read them. Marie Clay, perhaps the greatest reading researcher of all time, often told us that one of the best ways to ensure that children are ready to take off as conventional readers—reading level C and above books—is to be sure that they write texts that we can read and they can read. Those texts can contain patches of prose that are undecipherable; if the child can put his or her finger under the print and read most of the text, then that youngster is ready to take off as a conventional reader.

Many of the kindergarten teachers we know best aim to move kids into actual reading—of simple books, with one-to-one matching—by about December. This unit, then, is called *Writing for Readers* not only because children write texts that their friends can read but also because this writing work sets up children to become readers. The unit allows them to make dramatic progress in their early reading behaviors so that they are able to read with one-to-one matching, using sight words to anchor their reading, drawing on phonics, syntax, and meaning to solve words.

The writing standard that asks kindergartners to "narrate a single event or several loosely related events, tell about the events in the order in which they occurred, and provide a reaction to what happened" (CCSS W.K.3) is our building block for this unit. We'll revisit it often and extend our expectations and teaching beyond it as well. In fact, the unit aims to support kindergarteners to move toward meeting the CCSS (W.1.3) standard for first grade.

The unit also helps writers monitor for meaning and notice when a text—in this case, their own writing—doesn't make sense.

"Teaching kids to give their own writing an 'Is this easy to read?' test helps them internalize what makes texts readable."

Today you will ask the children to divide their writing into piles—one of Easy to Read and one of Hard to Read writing. The children will share why some texts were in the hard to read pile and will collect thoughts about what's necessary for writing to be readable. You will be trying to hand over an awareness of what makes texts readable. Research by John Hattie and others has shown that all learners progress most quickly when they have crystal clear images of what it is they aim to achieve. Teaching kids to give their own writing an "Is this easy to read?" test helps them to internalize what makes texts readable.

Writing for Readers

CONNECTION

Celebrate the growth in your students' writing thus far, and rally them around the prospect of working really hard and making their writing get even better.

"Writers, when you come to the meeting area, you will see your writing folder. Sit on your folder please." Once all the children had found their spots, I began. "Writers, do you remember the story I told you about the giraffe measuring stick that my mother had? And how on each birthday, I had to stand as tall as possible against that measuring stick, heels up against the wall. Then my mother would figure out my height and write my name and the date at that place on the measuring stick. And remember how I told you that what was so cool about that giraffe was that all these years later I can still look back at the markings on that giraffe and think, 'Wow! I was once *that* little? I can't believe how much I grew!' I'm telling you this because yesterday's celebration was almost a writers' birthday. You weren't ending *a year* of your *life* but *a unit* of your *writing* life. That means that today, like all birthdays, is a good time to notice how much you have grown.

"I wish I had a giraffe measuring stick stuck to this easel, and I could ask each of you to stand, heels back, head high, so we could mark how tall you have grown. But the real goal is to think how you have grown *as a writer*, and the best way to think about that is to look between the first piece of writing you made at the start of this year and the story you just published, and to think, 'How have I changed?' Will you and your partner each take your writing out, and will you show each other what your writing was like at the very start of this year, and what it has been like more recently, and will you talk about how you have changed as a writer?" I gave the students some time to look through their folders and share with each other.

After a few minutes, I reconvened the group. "On our imaginary giraffe measuring stick, your writing went from being toe-high to knee-high! I've been thinking and thinking about what I can teach you next so that after our *next* authors' celebration, when you lay your first piece of writing out and again look to see how much you have grown, it will be like—Holy moly! A miracle!"

Fullan reminds us that all we do as teachers needs to be powered by a sense of moral imperative. The job is to accelerate students' progress. This minilesson begins with you looking kids in the eyes and saying, "The whole purpose of all this is to support your growth."

When children look back on their work, contrasting the caliber of their work at the start of the year with their work six weeks later and they see dramatic improvements in that work, this sets the trajectory and tells children, "Your work is getting better by leaps and bounds. I can't wait to see how much better it is by next week!"

FIG. 1–1

Build students' energy for challenging themselves to make their stories even better.

"How many of you think that if you have more time to write stories, and if you can help each other and look at books to get ideas for making your stories even better, you can go from writing that is this good," I made a knee-high gesture, "to writing that is this good?" and I reached above my head.

The children all seemed confident. "It is going to take hard work," I said and made muscles in my arms, as if I were a weight lifter. "I have been thinking and thinking about what I can teach you that will help. I have decided to tell you about something that happened to me Friday night."

I'm referring to the evening after our last author's celebration.

Tell a detailed story of trying to read your children's writing. Share your great yearning to read their stories and your frustration when you couldn't.

"After our celebration on Friday, I couldn't bear to leave your writing in school so I brought it home with me. I started watching TV, and then I said, 'Wait a minute. Why am I watching TV when I have my kids' stories at home?' I thought, 'My kids' stories would be so much better than this show!' So I turned off the TV, and I got the box of your writing, and some tea and a blanket, and I wrapped myself up and snuggled down to read, like this." I reenacted the utter bliss of the moment and showed how I reached for a story. "I started to read." Turning to the first page of a dummy chart-sized book I'd made of an imaginary child's writing, I pointed at the words and read, "Me and my sister went on the ropes."

Take the time to paint a scene, to recreate the image of you, snuggling down to read your children's work. Your longing to read what your children have written will become the force behind this whole unit. This is not window dressing, it's crucial! Play up your involvement in the first section of this story so that your children empathize when you encounter difficulties and can't read on.

ME ND MI SITER WNT ON DA ROPS

Still acting the part of my Friday-night-reading self, I said, "Oh, I can't wait to see what happens next!" Turning the page, I read, touching the print as I decoded it, "We climbed the bumps. We went high."

WE CIMD DA BMPS. WE WNT HI

Turning to the final page, I looked at the print, my finger under the words, and then stopped in my tracks. I stared more closely at the page, baffled.

In a moment like this, ham things up. Let the kids see you try, try, try. "Oh, no! Oh, dear! What to do . . . ?"

WIGSDNR DADHSDN.

Recalling the storyline, I said, "You were climbing high . . . and then what happened?" and again I peered at the string of letters.

Turning back through the pages, I reread and retold the cliffhanger of a story, this time letting my intonation show the rising suspense. "Oh my gosh! They were on the rope. They had climbed up the bumps, the knots, and they were high. And . . . And . . . wigsdnr? I'm left hanging!"

Now stepping back out of the role playing, I said to the class, "I had to stop reading this great story without learning how it ended because I couldn't read it." I spoke with woe. "I was so sad that the writer hadn't written in a way that let me read the whole story. Let's start our new unit today by saying that if writers work really hard and help each other, then every writer can make it so that people can read his or her story. That will be our project for the next unit—to write so people can read our writing."

❖ Name the teaching point.

"Today I want to teach you that writers use all their writing muscles to make sure people don't put their writing down. Like all writers, each of you can tell if your writing is easy to read by reading *your own writing* like it's a book in your book baggie. If you can't figure out what your writing says, then you need to fix it up so other people won't have the same trouble."

TEACHING

Tell children that they'll want to shift from writing to reading their own stories, and caution them that they'll need to invest some extra work in that reading.

"So writers, today you will be able to write another true story, from your life. And today and every day when you write a story, you will want to stop in the middle of your writing and pretend it is reading time and that the book that you are writing is one of the books in your book baggie. Then you get your own writing out of your imaginary baggie and read it, just like you read all those books during reading time.

"But here is a tip. The book won't be finished. A publishing company will not have fixed it up yet and added perfect pictures and everything. Your writing is what writers call 'rough draft writing.' And whenever a writer rereads rough draft writing, the writer has to do some extra work to read the words and the pictures."

Show children that when reading their stories, you use the pictures to help you guess what the words say, and you also point under the print and use word-solving strategies.

"Let me show you what I did at home last night when I really, really, *really* wanted to read your writing. Pretend I'm at home, and I have a wonderful stack of your stories right here. Watch—this is what I did to read your writing." I got one child's writing and looked at it. I didn't show the piece to the class but did hold it in my lap and then visibly pulled closer to peer at it. "Oh yeah, that shows Shawn on his bike," I said, pointing at part of the picture. "I don't know who this person in the picture is, but it *might* be Anthony, his brother. So maybe the story will say 'bike' and maybe it will say 'Anthony.' "

Pausing, I said to the class, "Think in your mind what I just did." I left a little thought time.

Research by Hattie has shown that learners accelerate their progress when they have a crystal clear sense of their goals. Our hope is that we're stirring children to know and care about the goal of this unit.

Notice that writing so people can read the story is depicted as a matter of muscle. Most children know that people can work hard to strengthen their muscles, so this is suggesting that all writers can reach this goal.

Of course, the really unfinished element in students' writing will be the spelling.

This may strike you as tough, even brutal. "Why confront five-year-olds with the fact that their writing is hard to read?" you ask. We think that kids need to be willing to work hard to spell in ways that make their writing readable, and that transparency helps.

Continuing, I said, "Now let me try to read the words." (Then, turning to the class, I stage whispered, "I copied them up here on the easel.") As I said this, I displayed the enlarged writing on the easel and put my finger under the first word. "'*I rd.*' Hmm. What could that say? '*I rd* (?)'" I continued reading, giving the class a look that signaled that I hoped they noticed this strategy. Again, I touched the print, "'*mi bik*?' Oh! I got it. '*I rode my bike*.'" I reread again to be sure, "I rode my bike" and gestured to the drawing, saying, "Yep, that matches."

Recruit the class to join you in naming the strategies they saw you using to read hard-to-read writing.

Then, turning to the group, I asked, "What did you notice me doing when I *really* wanted to read Shawn's story?" The group agreed that I had used the picture and all I knew about Shawn to help, and that I'd pointed under the words and read on when I was stuck and read with an "I bet I can figure this out" attitude. Most of all, I hadn't given up.

Nodding, I said, "I can read this writing! I am going to make two piles of my writing—one pile of Easier to Read (I could call it Possible to Read) and one pile of Really Hard (even Impossible) to Read. I'm going to put this piece in the Easier to Read pile over here. If I get one that I *can't* read, even when I try as hard as I just tried, then I'm going to put it in my Really Hard to Read pile."

Notice that I don't record this list. If you chart everything, you aren't helping children distinguish the truly important content. More charts are not necessarily better.

ACTIVE ENGAGEMENT

Ask the children to read through the writing in their own folders and make two piles, the more and the less readable writing.

"Right now, I would like every writer in here to open your folder and find your most recent story. And will you work really hard to read the first page of that writing? I want to see your fingers under the first word. You are going to look at it and think, 'What *could* this say?' Remember, you can look at the picture to see if that gives you some clues. If you finish reading one page, you can go to the next page."

As children read, I moved quickly among them, pointing out to some whose writing was especially Hard to Read that looking at the picture can help, and that sometimes when rereading writing, writers get the idea that we better add more letters. "If your writing has no words, don't feel badly. It'll just go in the Really Hard to Read pile. Everyone is going to have one of those piles.

"I'm noticing that some of you have finished reading your first pieces. Now you can go back to the other stories you already wrote that are in your folder and try *really hard* to read those stories. Some of your writing came from the very, very start of the year, and it will be *hard* to read, and there will probably be some pieces that are *easier* to read. Put your writing in piles: an Easier to Read or a Really Hard to Read pile."

Remember that youngsters have their folders full of work they did during the previous unit in front of them.

Ask the children to share their piles with a friend, talking together about *why* one pile is hard to read and the other is easier.

After no more than two minutes, I spoke over the hubbub, saying "Now writers, I know you aren't finished, but will you and your partner talk about what makes a piece of writing easier or harder to read?"

Soon animated conversations were under way. Not surprisingly, the children didn't necessarily talk about what writing was hard or easy to read, but instead, they talked about their abilities to write conventionally. Daniel announced to Lilly, "I only have one pile. She said we need two piles. I don't have no Easy to Read writing."

Lilly shrugged. "I am almost the same as you, but I got one story my mom did with me at home. It was easy 'cause my mom spelled the words."

This seemed like a good idea to Daniel, who said, "My dad is good at words, like your mom. I can make my writing good, too."

Debrief in ways that recruit children to be ready to work like the dickens so their writing becomes easy to read.

Overhearing this, I said to the class, "Writers, I heard some of you say your parents can be good helpers. That's *one* way you could make your writing easier to read—by asking someone to spell the words for you. If your parents help you too much, though, you won't be practicing. During this unit, you are going to learn to help yourself. Remember that right now, you might feel as if you are not that good at writing Easier to Read Writing. You might be at the giraffe's toes. But in a few weeks—you'll see—this will change!"

LINK

Send children off to continue dividing their writing into Hard to Read and Easy to Read piles, figuring out what makes writing belong in one pile or another.

"Writers, today, instead of starting right away to write a new story, do you first want to spend a little more time, going back to the stories you already wrote that are in your folder and trying *really hard* to read that writing? Some of your writing came from the very, very start of the year, and it will be *hard* (or impossible) to read, and there will probably be some pieces that are *easier* to read. Put your writing in piles: an Easy to Read pile and a Hard to Read pile."

The children all signaled that they'd be happy to do that. "I've put paper clips and Post-it® notes on your table so that once you have your writing in piles, you can clip all the Hard to Read pieces together and name that pile, and do the same for the Easy to Read pile. *Then* . . . you know what we are going to do? We are going to try to figure out why some writing is Hard to Read and why some is Easy to Read."

Pace is important. The point is not for kids to finish rereading their pieces. The goal is simply for them to get a taste of reading pieces that are hard to read, noting what makes them hard.

Imagine every child in the room turning to talk with his or her friend, and me crouching among the pairs of children, listing in on their conversations. Very often I draw from what I hear in these partnership conversations to cite one example of the sort of thing I hope children are saying. I would never ask child after child to report on what they said to each other.

It's helpful to thread earlier bits of a minilesson into later portions of the minilesson.

Teachers, if it appears to you that many children will not be able to read much of what they have written, you may decide to not use some of your writing time for this rereading work, in which case you can skip immediately to the first mid-workshop teaching, which would help you channel kids to start right off today writing stories that are easier for people to read.

Multitasking to Get the Unit Up and Going

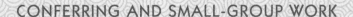

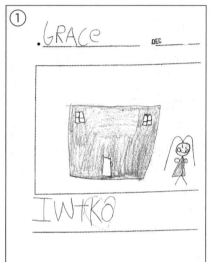

AT THE START OF ANY UNIT, it will be important for you to put on your roller skates and move quickly among children. The nature of this unit is such that it will be harder for you to roller-skate quickly among your kids, making sure they are all engaged in the work of this unit because you'll be challenging students to focus on the aspect of writing that is hard for them. The unit is about working with the hard stuff—with letters and sounds. There is a way then, in which not all of your kids will be needy. This means it will be especially important for you to prioritize.

Your first goal, then, will simply be to get children working together in partnerships to reread the writing they've written previously in the year. Make sure children are helping each other, with a piece of writing held between them, and the two of them working together to read the piece, trying and trying again. Make sure the children are pointing under the words, scrutinizing the picture, thinking about what the words could mean. Even if the piece seems very hard to read, it would be great if you could encourage children to give the text their careful attention.

As you make sure the class is engaged, leave time for children who know that their writing is not as readable as it could be. It will help you to understand the reasons for this problem. Sometimes the source of the problem will be a child's nervousness to write unknown words. Sometimes it will be that the child hears only the starting or the ending sounds in a word, strings words together into what appears to be a random string of letters, or actually does no sounding at all and just writes a page of letters.

Although you will be interested in detecting the deeper reasons for the problem, the work you need to do with one group of writers and another will not be all that different for now. The most immediate thing will be that some of these children could be feeling really lousy because you just ripped away any illusion that it is okay to just pretend-write. You also ripped away any illusion that their approximations were totally fine. You'll need to turn discouragement into resolve. First of all, if some children are realizing they can't read any of their writing, you will want to support their awareness of this. Although it is not great that they haven't written texts that are readable, it *is*

FIG. 1–2   Grace's Costco story. I went to Costco. We bought snacks. We bought food.

Once I detected that a fair percentage of the class was ready to move from rereading their old writing to making some new writing, I stood in the midst of the hubbub and said, "Writers! Eyes up here." After I had their attention, I continued. "Writers, many of you have read over a lot of your writing, and I hear you saying that a lot of your writing is hard to read. That's a great thing to realize! But it is going to be even more helpful if you think about *why* it is hard to read, because that will give you some ideas for what you could do to fix it up. I'm wondering, can you and your partner talk about what makes your writing hard to read, so we can start to make a list?" Before long, I again called for children's attention, and this time, they contributed to a list, which I scrawled onto chart paper.

What Makes Writing Hard
to Read
the letters are smushed together   girl
not many letters   t.ble

What Makes Writing Easy to Read
spaces ("it isn't all scrunched together") girl
neat ("without a lot of eraser marks") clean
a lot of letters in every word   tables
pictures that help   sun

"Writers, we still have time for writing. I don't know about all of you, but whenever I read through my old writing, I always get inspired to pick up my pencil and make some new writing. Do you feel that way, too?" I checked for nods and thumbs up. "Now that you've spent some time thinking about what makes your writing *hard* to read or *easy* to read, I'm wondering if you think you can write a new story, and this time make it as easy to read as possible?" The children seemed up for that. "Think about something you do, maybe something you did at home last night or over the weekend." I was quiet, letting them think. "Tell your partner what you could write about in a new story. Turn and talk."

After a minute, I said, "Guys, would some of you share your story ideas?"

Lilly raised her hand and said, "My aunt had a birthday party yesterday, and we danced." "Good one," I said. "You gotta write that one!"

Michael called, "We did laundry and found a spider in the machine." "Awww," I groaned. "You gotta write that one!"

"How about when my hat blew down the street in the wind, and we chased it?" Riley offered, and again I insisted that it was a must.

"So many great true stories. You can get started writing your new story. Remember to think of something you have done, and to start by touching the pages, telling the story. Then sketch—and write!"

a big step forward that they realize this. And it is okay that the youngster is sad about not being able to read his or her writing. After all, your goal is for children to want to write so that others can read their writing and to be willing to work toward this goal. So yes, you are asking them to look at the writing and to say, with some sadness, "I bet *no one* can read this!" And then your goal is to transform discouragement into resolve so that children do more to help their readers.

Once children have faced the fact that their writing is hard to read, you'll want to help them turn this around—and actually, helping children write more readable writing is what most of your conferences over the next few days will entail. In those conferences, you will help the writer hear and record a sound, and then the next sound. Coach the child to say a word, isolate the first sound, find and record letters to match that sound, then to reread, and then articulate the entire word again, to hear the next sound. Once the child has written the complete word, you'll say, "Read it. Put your finger under the

word and read it." The child will be able to do this, and then you, as well, can read the word. "You are writing readable writing!" you'll say, congratulating the child, then getting him or her started on the next word. Once the child has started saying that word, identifying the first sound and recording it, you'll need to slip away, knowing that chances are good that without your help, the child will hear fewer sounds, will produce something less readable. But your instruction won't take the child from A to Z, and it is big work that you are engaging children to work with great resolve, trying to write readable writing.

That work, described earlier, is slow. It will require you to stay at a writer's side for four or five minutes and to actually coach into the child's efforts. One of your challenges, then, will be to get around to and spend some time getting with all your children while also spending time conducting this intensive and slow type of a conference. One answer is to sometimes conduct conferences such as the one described earlier with a small group watching. You can tell all the children, "I'm going to teach Abby how to write readable writing, and she'll do her work on this giant piece of chart paper so you all can watch. Then afterward, I'll help all of you get started doing the same thing that I teach Abby to do." Then, in the midst of your conference, often while the child is working at something, you'll look up to the ring of observing children and point out what you hope they are noticing.

Although the unit brings in a new focus on writing conventionally, the last thing you want is for children to become so intent on spelling that they forget that their big goal is to write true stories, drawing and telling what happened first, next, and next. This means that throughout the unit, a fair share of your conferences and small groups will support narrative writing. You'll want to help children think about all the things that they do, to isolate one of those micro-events, and to tell that as a story. Although you aren't emphasizing focusing those stories so the child is writing about a small

moment, the truth is that when a child writes about an event that occurred within fifteen minutes rather than four days, the story is far more apt to contain detail, dialogue, and description. So you might conduct conferences in which you say, "Instead of writing about the whole day at the fair, can you think of one particular thing you did that you especially want to tell about in this story? How did that start? What exactly were you doing at the start of that?" Then, once the child retells the start of a particular ride at the fair, for example, you can say, "Oh my goodness, you should definitely put that on your first page. Draw it, quickly, and then touch that page, tell that part of the story, and go on to the next page."

Although most of your conferences in this session will help writers record sounds, your real message will be that writers plan out great stories and then use letter-sound knowledge to write in ways others can read.

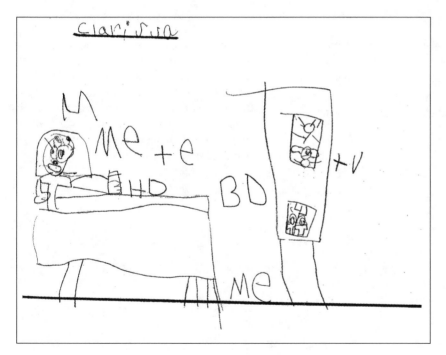

FIG. 1–3

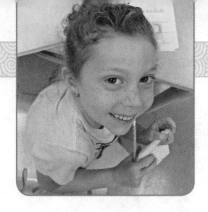

Highlighting One Student's Successful Work

Tell the children about a writer who did something to make his or her writing more readable.

"Hey everyone, today Juliser did the coolest thing. Juliser finished writing the first page of her story, and she realized that she could not read what she had written. So she started her writing over again. She just crossed out what she'd written—the part she couldn't read—and this time, after she wrote a little bit, *she reread her own writing*. Then she wrote some more and *then* she *reread her writing again* like this. She made her next draft easy to read by rereading it often. Watch how she did it."

I had quickly made an enlarged copy of the start of Juliser's story on chart paper. Stepping into the role of Juliser, I put my finger under the letters *me* and reenacted Juliser reading that word and articulating what she wanted to write next: "Me *and*." I wrote *and*, gesturing to the word wall, and went back to reread "Me *and*." Soon I'd voiced "mommy" and had written an approximation of that. "I bet a lot of you found ways to make sure that your writing is easy to read. How many of you wrote in ways that will help me read your writing?" Across the room, children signified that yes, indeed, they'd done this. "I'll be taking your stories home tonight and I can't wait to read them."

Notice how I don't just talk about what Juliser did. I reenact it. That is, instead of giving an explanation, I give a demonstration. The demonstration is deliberately tailored to highlight the one thing I want to emphasize, which is the process Juliser went through as she voiced the word she wanted to write, isolated a sound, recorded it, reread, and then voiced it again.

How to Write True Stories that Readers Really Want to Read

IN THE SHARE SESSION that capped yesterday's workshop, you told children you couldn't wait to read the writing that they made the preceding day. Those words need to actually be true. This unit requires that you are watching the effect your teaching has on your students. The risk is that by asking for very young children to write more conventionally, you could inadvertently raise the stakes too high, too quickly.

I will never forget when I decided my lawn had too many dandelions on it, so I spread weed killer liberally across the lawn—and ended up with very little lawn at all. Likewise, you don't want your good intentions to be too ambitious, too quickly. You are hoping to create growing pains—but not ones that are toxic!

One way to moderate the risk of focusing too much on the importance of writing more readable writing is to make sure that you help children write true stories while *also* helping them make those stories more readable. In this book, we will be devoting the majority of minilessons to helping children write in such a way that others can read their writing, but you may decide to moderate that emphasis with quite a few minilessons that aim to support narrative writing. If you decide to teach more minilessons on narrative craft than those we have provided, you can always convert the narrative craft advice we give in the conferring and small-group sections into full-class minilessons. Alternatively, you can borrow a first-grade teacher's Small Moments book and adapt a few of those minilessons to suit your kindergartners, interspersing them into this unit.

For the next few sessions, you'll bring forward the chart that children relied upon to support their narrative writing during the *Launch the Writing Workshop* unit into this session, and you will make it explicit to children that while they are working to make readable stories, they also need to remember and draw upon all they know about writing true stories. In Bend II, we'll introduce the formal narrative checklist students used at the end of the *Launch* unit.

Some of your children are already aware that they have stories to tell; they just forget those stories sometimes when faced with the empty page. These are the youngsters

IN THIS SESSION, you'll teach students that writers call upon what they have already learned. Specifically, you'll teach them how to go back to old anchor charts on narrative writing and use them in their new writing.

GETTING READY

✔ "How to Write a True Story," from the *Launching the Writing Workshop* unit (see Teaching and Share)

✔ Enlarged blank story booklet, made from chart paper (see Teaching)

✔ Clipboards with pens attached

✔ Student copies of "How to Write a True Story" (see Teaching)

✔ Student writing folders (see Connection)

✔ Enlarged page from a blank story booklet, made from chart paper (see Mid-Workshop Teaching)

COMMON CORE STATE STANDARDS: W.K.3, W.1.3, RFS.K.1, SL.K.1, L.K.1, L.K.2, L.1.2.e

who run into your classroom after a weekend, bursting with, "Ooooh, ooooohs" and "I gotta tell you somethings." Of course, when it is time for writing workshop, those stories can hide, and you'll help writers find them.

"You will make it explicit to children that while they are working to make readable stories, they also need to remember and draw upon all they know about writing true stories."

But there are other children in your class who probably do not come to school bursting with stories to tell. These children may say to you, "I didn't do anything this weekend," and they may say, "Nothing happens in my life." You will want to help these writers realize that there are stories everywhere. Almost nothing else can transform your workshop more than teaching your writers how to find the moments that matter.

Once your children begin to know how to find these stories for themselves, they will also be able to help their classmates find them, too. You will know your writers are doing this for each other when they say something like, "Hey, you should make that into a booklet," not just during writing time but also in the hallway or during a science experiment.

As this unit unfolds, you will return to the anchor chart, "How to Write a True Story," periodically to remind children of everything that writers do when they attempt to write true stories.

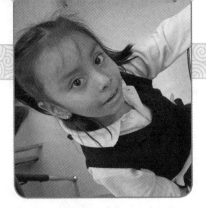

How to Write True Stories that Readers Really Want to Read

CONNECTION

Praise students for working so hard to make their writing easy to read.

"Writers, bring your folders and let's meet," I said, and once the children had convened, I began. "When I took your writing home last night, curled up with my blanket and my tea, and started to read your stories, guess what I found! I could read so much more of your writing! Many of you had said the word you wanted to write sl—ooooow—lllll—y, and isolated the first sound, /sssss/, and written that: *s.*" I wrote the *s* on chart paper as I spoke, and touched it to reread it. "Then you reread and said the word again sllllllllllowly and wrote the next sound! In that fashion, you recorded lots of sounds in your words.

"Right now, will you get out the writing you did yesterday, and put your finger under each word you wrote, starting with your name? See if you can figure out what each of the words says." The children did this for a minute.

"Do you see what I mean? Your writing is much easier to read! Give yourselves a pat on the back." They did this. "Now, sit up tall if you are ready for another hard job."

The children sat tall, and I nodded.

❖ Name the teaching point.

"Today I want to teach you that even when you are working really hard to hear all your sounds and to write so people can read your writing, you still need to remember everything you already learned about writing great stories. It helps to reread old charts, using those as reminders of all the things you can always remember to do."

TEACHING

Tell children that throughout the upcoming unit, they will write a new true story almost every day, and remind them that they know how to do this.

◆ COACHING

Units of study are meant to be a coherent, synthesized course of study. The references to prior instruction are tremendously important.

Whenever you can, use gestures to accompany your words. So when you describe students patting themselves on the back (and mean celebrating accomplishments), act it out—this helps kids who listen better when there are visuals accompanying the oral language, and it especially helps your English language learners.

Whenever it is writing workshop during the next few weeks, you are going to be able to write *another* true story. And here is the important thing: I'm not going to be teaching you how to think up true stories from your life. I'm not going to teach you that you can remember what you did or said first and sketch that on your paper, and then sketch what you did or said. I'm not going to teach you how to do those things because," and I leaned in close and whispered, as if telling the class a secret, *"you already know how to do all that.*

"In this unit, I'm going to mostly teach you how to spell your words and how to leave spaces between your words and to use punctuation like," and I made a period and a question mark and an exclamation mark. "But *you* will not just be spelling words and leaving spaces and punctuating—you will be writing true stories. On Monday, you will write a true story. And then on Tuesday, you will—that's right, you will write a true story. On Wednesday, what will you do? Write a true story. And no one will tell you how to write true stories because," again I leaned in, as if to tell a secret, this time hoping the children would chime in, *"you already know how."*

Role-play that you are a kindergartner wanting to write, doing this in a way that channels children to reread the first two points of the "How to Write a True Story" chart.

"So let's say it is writing time today, and I say, 'Off you go, get started,' and you go to your writing spot and sit down." I acted these things out, getting up, walking in a circle, sitting in my chair as if I am now a kindergartner." What will you do first? I guess, you get a story booklet, right?"

I got an enlarged one, made of chart paper. "Now what? Oh no! What do I write about?" After a pause, I said, "Here is a tip. You can look back at the chart from our last unit to remind yourself of what to do. And the cool thing is that I made each of you your own copy of this chart. You can add tips to yourself on your private copy of this chart, and you can keep it with you every day as you write." I passed out the private copies of the charts, each clipped to a clipboard with a pen attached.

> ### How to Write a True Story
>
> - Think of something that happened or that you did.
> - Tell what happened with pictures and words.
>   - Tell WHO is in the story.
>   - Tell WHERE the story takes place.
>   - Tell WHAT is happening.
> - Practice telling the story in a storyteller's voice.
> - Use speech bubbles to remember what people said.

"I'm going to mark up our class chart, and you can mark your copy of the chart the same way, or you can leave yours as it is. That is up to you." I grabbed a marker and wrote the number one next to the first bullet point on the chart. I said,

Think about your own learning. It's helpful, isn't it, if the Unit of Study book gives you the broad overlay of the course of study, the bigger goals, the timetables—all of this puts control into your hands. That is our aim here.

Strategies are only useful if there's trouble. If there is no trouble, one proceeds on automatic pilot. In this role play, you become a kindergartner who is stuck, who isn't sure how to proceed when writing the story, so that you can show children that in those instances you reach for the help of a chart and then use the chart to help you accomplish the goal.

"So whenever I want to write a new story. I need to think of something important that happened. I need to think about one moment I think will make a really good story."

Specifically, add on the fact that when choosing a story idea, it helps to feel excited about the story you elect to tell.

"You know, the other day, I told Aiden that true stories are better if they are 'Oooh, oooh' stories. 'Oooh, oooh' stories are stories that you can't wait to tell. I am going to add a drawing to my chart that has kids saying, like Aiden suggested, 'Ooooh, ooooh,' like, 'Ooooh, I have a good story.' I am going to make sure that the kids have excited looks on their faces like you all do when you have a story that you are dying to tell someone." I added some drawings onto my chart. Some children did the same on their individual charts.

"I'm thinking of an 'Oooh, oooh' story that I can write. I have one. Last night I hunted for the right size for a shoe for a long time. I almost gave up! Then I found it—and look!" I showed my shoes to everyone.

ACTIVE ENGAGEMENT

Ask children to tell you what you'd do next, if you are trying to write a true story, and then do the first two steps—thinking of and storytelling a story—to prepare for the day's writing.

"Will you all see if you can use the chart to decide what I need to do next? Work with your partner and see if you can make a suggestion for me. GO!"

In no time, the children produced the idea that I needed to decide what happens first in my book. I nodded. "You are right, but hey, I don't want to be the only one following this chart. Right now, will you follow step 1 and step 2? That means you need to think of an 'Oooh, oooh' story, and you need to tell what happens first in the story. Then, you need to tell what happens next. Remember when you story-tell your story, you'll want to tell it across your fingers." I held up my fist and popped up a first finger as I said, "I found a great sweatshirt at the store." I popped up a second finger and continued, "I was too small, so I looked and looked for my size. After you think of a story you can tell about something you did, tell it with details. Go!"

LINK

Remind children that when they disperse to their writing places, they'll refer to their individual charts of how to write true stories for guidance.

"So writers, in a minute I am going to say, 'Off you go.' And then you will get up and walk to your writing place, and you will get started writing a true story about something that happened to you. Remember when you plan, you draw your story first using your three planning pages. Show me the chart that you are going to look at if you get stuck and do not know what to do." The children waved their charts high. "Okay. Here goes! Off you go."

Note that the "Oooh, oooh" story is one of hunting for and finding the missing shoe. The message is clear: the true details of life matter.

We'd originally written this to say, "I found some great shoes at the store. They were too small," but when we give examples, we try to make them different, one from the next so as to open up possibilities for children. We'd just talked about an "Oooh, oooh" story being "I lost my shoe... I looked for it for a long time..." so now, at the store we substituted sweatshirt for shoe.

Support the Whole Process of Narrative Writing

IN MANY COOKING RECIPES, there is this bit of instruction: "Add flour slowly, stirring all the while." This session reminds you that when you are making not bread but writers, the recipe continues to call for a gradual addition. "Add conventions slowly, stirring all the while." Too much of a preoccupation on spelling and punctuation, poured in at too fast a clip, can clog up everything. So today's session reminds you that you need to balance your attention to conventions with an attention to narrative writing and to the writing process in general.

Upcoming conferring write-ups will provide you with detailed help supporting children's growing abilities to hear and record sounds, to rely on sight words, and to alternate between writing and rereading. This conferring write-up will focus on the conferences and small-group work that you'll do in order to sustain children's interest in writing narratives. In actuality, on any given day's workshop, you will spend some of your time conferring around phonics and conventions and some around narrative writing.

One way to think about the conferring and small-group work you will do to support narrative writing is to consider what children will tend to do during each part of the writing process: early, later, and toward the end. It is somewhat helpful to anticipate that as long as children are writing a story a day (which is about usual when children are so young), then at the start of any day's writing workshop you will tend to support students in creating legible writing or in generating ideas for and rehearsing true stories. Then later during any day's writing workshop, you will tend to help children actually draft their stories. Toward the end of any day's workshop, you will be more apt to support children in either finding ways to end their stories or rereading and revising those stories. Then there is a predictable rhythm to the work you do each day in workshop.

When helping your youngsters generate idea for narrative writing, it will be important for you to lower the bar enough so that every child can do this without needing your help. It can actually be very demanding to select a perfect story idea. If you try to write a true story from your life, you probably will find that selecting the story idea can be half the battle. Keep in mind that this is challenging for you because you put your ideas to the test: Does the idea matter to me? Does it feel like a coherent story? and so forth. Your children, however, don't have enough experience writing to be apt to take in so many considerations. Instead, they recall something they did—they ate breakfast—and presto: a topic!

This minilesson tries to raise the stakes just a bit, suggesting the story needs to be one the writer wants to tell. It is true the stories will be best if kids approach the page like shaken-up soda bottles, ready to explode. But if children are having trouble coming up with story ideas and are sitting around doing nothing as a consequence, then lower

MID-WORKSHOP TEACHING
Hearing More Sounds in Labels and Sentences

"Writers, would you look up, please? Each of you knows the kind of work you are practicing when it comes to writing words that tell your story. If you are stretching words and putting the first sound you hear into labels in your pictures, that's great. Make sure you have lots of labels on each page."

Then I added, "Some of you are stretching words to hear ending sounds, too. Would each of you make sure you are doing that in your labels?" Nodding, from me and the children. "Hear sounds at the start of the word, and then hear the middle of the word, and then the end.

"And some of you are moving from labels to sentences. If you have been writing labels that people can read, you can graduate to sentences! Go back to work."

your standards and help them realize that *anything* can become a story, as long as the writer tells what happens first, next, and last. And actually, the writer need only sketch this, for starts, making the entire prospect of writing far less awe inspiring. If you notice that you have several children who chronically struggle to come up with ideas and thus spend half of their writing time staring at a blank page, perhaps you will convene a small group immediately after your minilesson. Perhaps you will share a strategy you use for generating topics. Maybe you will have a little storytelling circle, giving students an opportunity to listen to the ideas of others. Either way, do not send them off to their writing until they have come up with an idea to get started on.

If you have helped children use strategies to generate story ideas and they still do not get started, sometimes it helps to ask them to draw themselves. Then ask them to think about where they are and what they might be doing in the picture. "Draw that," I say. Sometimes just getting your pencil moving (instead of *trying to come up with a true story idea*) is the very thing stuck writers need.

Once a child has sketched and story-told a story (pointing at a page while story-telling it), then you'll want to help the writer write the story. "Say it. Write it," you'll say. As you confer at this point in the process, be sure you channel children toward work that is readily doable for them. Some of your children are not yet writing beginning, middle, and ending sounds to words, so you will want those children to spend time

labeling their drawings. Later in this unit, you'll move even these more novice children toward writing in sentences. By this time in the year, an increasing number of your kindergarten children should be writing with beginning and ending sounds anyhow, and we think those children profit from being asked to produce sentences underneath the drawing on each page in their book. Pull these children into a small group. Model with your own writing or a shared writing sample. You can even work fishbowl style, sitting beside one student as you coach him to add sentences to his writing, all the while asking the others in the group to observe.

Some of the time, as children do this, you will be helping with spelling and spaces between words. Balance that by also spending time helping children clarify and convey the story. "Say it. Write it," you'll say. If writers can handle more suggestions, encourage them to picture what happened and to write what happened exactly. Details are everything when writing. What exactly did you do, say, eat, or think? People want to be able to picture it.

You may tend to think that these children are just five years old so revision is out of their reach, but actually, when playing in blocks, children revise constantly. They can be reminded to do so when they write as well. "Reread your story and think, 'Does that make any sense?'" For little children, most revision involves adding on, and kids profit from being taught to use arrows or slips of extra paper to make this process easier.

I went to McDonald's with my sister.

FIG. 2–1

We were eating hamburgers.

My sister's hamburger fell on the floor.

Keeping Track of One's Progress

Teach students how to use the "How to Write a True Story" chart to self-assess and make plans for future writing.

"Writers, I am so proud of the work you have been doing, planning and writing true stories. I thought now it would be a good idea to think about the work you need to do the *next* time you sit down and write. Remember, writers make plans! Now, you all brought a piece of writing that you have been working on, right? Let me see it!" The students hold their writing in the air, waving it around for me to see.

"Let's take a look at the chart. I'll read through the things on this list, and if you did those things in the piece of writing you have with you, give a thumbs up. And if you didn't do it yet, and you'll do it next time, thumbs down. Ready?" I read through each item on the list slowly, giving the students a chance to self-assess their writing.

"Now that you've had a chance to go through the chart of how to write a true story, turn to your partner and tell him or her what your plan is for tomorrow. Which things did you give yourself a thumbs down for? If you gave yourself a thumbs up for many things that you did from this list, you are probably done with that story for now. If you are done, you can put that story on the finished side of your folder. If there are some things on the list that you still want to try on a story, you can keep it on the unfinished side of your folder. You'll be able to come back to this next time!"

> ### How to Write a True Story
>
> - Think of something that happened or that you did.
> - Practice telling the story in a storyteller's voice.
> - With pictures and words
>   - Tell **who** is in the story.
>   - Tell **where** the story takes place.
>   - Tell **what** is happening.
> - Use speech bubbles to show what people said.

FIG. 2–2

Drawing Stories for Readers

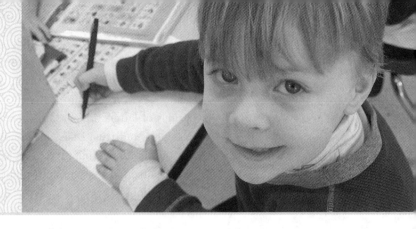

THIS MINILESSON WILL FOCUS ON DRAWING PICTURES that readers can read. Your instinct may be to do just the opposite—to move youngsters to invest more and more of their time in labels and captions. You are right to want to channel children to write more and more words, but the truth is that for beginning writers, drawing more and more representationally can sometimes be one way to support writing more letters and words. When pictures are representational enough and detailed enough that they tell and hold a story, the picture essentially provides the writer with a way to hold his content, his thought, long enough that he can toil away at putting that content into letters, sounds, words. Beginning writers, like beginning readers, use pictures to help them make meaning and generate language. So a lesson or two on drawing representationally is a way to encourage writers to write more conventionally.

Although this minilesson spotlights drawing, children will be writing whole stories. The work you did at the start of the unit on writing Easy to Read stories will still be very much in the air. By helping children know that one way to make stories easy to read is to make the drawings "match" the child's mental image, you give every child a way to succeed at the work of this unit. And you allow children to get going, drawing and writing what will hopefully be more readable stories.

Pay attention to those stories—both while kids are making them and afterward, when the kids have gone home and you are able to sit with collections of their work. Some of your writers will write stories using one- or two-word labels and pictures, while others will be writing sentences on each page. Some of their writing will be in an Easy to Read pile, and some, less easy. As you study the Hard to Read writing, you will want to work hard to decipher what the meaning could perhaps be. For example, a child may have drawn a house, with four spiderlike creatures near the front door, and under those spiderlike creatures, written this string of letters: *memdr*. Try to detect whether the clump of letters is all below one creature—a name?—or is the *me* below one figure, the *m* below another? If the latter is the case, could this perhaps say, *me*, *mom*, *dad*, and then the name of a sibling? That is, just as you teach kids that they need to work hard and not give up when trying

IN THIS SESSION, you'll elaborate on the process children use when they go about writing every day. You will teach children how to draw and talk about what they need in order to tell their story.

GETTING READY

✔ White boards and dry erase markers for each student (see Connection and Active Engagement)

✔ Chart paper, markers (see Teaching)

✔ "How to Write a True Story" chart, carried over from the *Launching the Writing Workshop* unit and Session 2 (see Teaching)

✔ Your shared class story from the teaching and active engagement, on chart paper (see Share)

COMMON CORE STATE STANDARDS: W.K.3, W.K.5, RL.K.1, RFS.K.7, SL.K.1, SL.K.5, SL.K.6, L.K.2.c,d to read a Hard to Read paper, *you*'ll also want to persevere, too. Chances are good that many pieces of writing that at first glance seem to contain just scribbled drawings and random strings of letters are actually more representational than you thought. Your trust that your children's writing does actually mean something, that there is logic to what they have written, will be an enormous gift and will help children live up to your expectations.

"Beginning writers, like beginning readers, use pictures to help them make meaning and generate language."

Of course, you are trying not only to read the story on the page but also to read the story of this writer. Might the consecutive circles be the result of a child enjoying the flow and colors of a marker pen? If it seems to have been hastily created, was the child rushing to make a whole pile of books? It is important for you to read children's work in this imaginative, inquisitive sort of a way, because you will want to develop a hypothesis about each of your children. These hypotheses will be based on very little information—it is not as if most five-year-olds can articulate the logic behind their work. That's okay. Just as a scientist begins an experiment by making a hypothesis, you'll want to begin this unit by making a hypothesis about each of your children as writers and as print people. Of course, children will fall into clusters. A few will seem to you to be so concerned about writing correctly that they copy words from their environment or ask incessantly for others to give them correct spelling. Others will seem to you to know all their letters but to have no real sense for how to tap that knowledge in order to write readable writing. Yet others will be able to sound out whole sentences but may not leave spaces between words.

The powerful thing is that your hunches about children will make you a vastly more powerful, efficient learner. You'll be looking to confirm or alter your hunch, and this will mean that everything you see kids actually doing will be especially interesting. It's great to approach writing time with hunches. As you see children in the act of writing, you can gather information that adds to or challenges your hunches. That is, two papers will contain what appears to be a random string of letters. Those papers look very much the same. But when you watch the writers in action, one writer says a word, locates a sound, says that sound repeatedly, records it, rereads it, then says the word, while another just sings la, la, la and spews a whole bunch of letters onto the page. When you watch writers at work, you'll see that two seemingly similar pieces of work in fact represent very different understandings about written language.

Drawing Stories for Readers

CONNECTION

Remind your class of the work of the unit, both by summarizing and by recruiting them to work on spelling one word.

I passed out white boards, with markers clipped to them, as children came to the meeting area. Once they were settled, I began. "Good morning, writers! I am so excited to be back together today to work on writing true stories that are easy to read. Yesterday, when you all used our chart about writing true stories to help you write, did some of you try to leave spaces between your words? Give me a thumbs up if you did that. *And* did some of you try to hear more sounds in a word and put down more letters? Thumbs up if you did that." The children so signaled. "Nice going.

"To get warmed up, let's work on our muscles for hearing all the letters in a word right now. Let's say you were telling a story about how your pencil broke and you had to write *pencil*. First, let's clap out the word 'pen-cil' and then say the first part, 'pen, pen.' Now, say that word slowly with your partner and see if you can help each other hear and record the first sound." I gave them a second to locate the /p/ sound and then did it for them. They all said /p/ and wrote that. "Fantastic, writers! Now go ahead and reread what you wrote, say the rest of the word, and keep going." I let them do this as best they could, on their own.

Note that children who get immersed in hearing letters and sounds (as your children will be as they work on spelling a word) sometimes have trouble remembering their story. Explain that today's lesson on drawing helps with that problem.

After the children worked on *pencil*, I reconvened them. "You know what sometimes happens, though? Sometimes writers spend so much time working on spelling one word—saying 'pencil' and hearing the /p/, then saying 'pencil' and hearing the /n/, that then we finish the one word and we think, 'Wait. What was I writing anyway?' Sometimes writers *forget* the whole story!

"But here is the thing. You know how when you are reading a book and you are not sure what the words say, you can check the picture and that helps you think of the story? The same is true when you are writing."

◆ COACHING

In many minilessons, the connection is a time when you recall what you have been teaching children, perhaps by rereading charts made on the previous days. This session accomplishes a similar job. A few days ago, you opened the unit by emphasizing that writers write readable stories, and you suggested that part of this involves the writer writing a word carefully, bit by bit, hearing and then recording all the sounds. Then you went on to focus on the accompanying challenge of writing true stories. This connection harkens back to the earliest work on writing readable stories. Instead of talking about that work, put it into action.

Name the teaching point.

"Today, I want to teach you that if you get so busy writing one word—like *pencil*—and you forget the whole story you wanted to write, you can look back up at your picture. The picture can remind you of the story, of all the words you wanted to write. *But* the picture helps you remember the story only if, when you made the picture, you were thinking about the words of the story."

TEACHING

Point out that before you draw a picture in a storybook, you first think of what it is that you did. Your picture records who did what, where writers say the words as they draw.

"I'm teaching you this because what I realized is that some of you guys draw pictures in your books *without thinking* about the words of your story as you draw! So maybe you wanted to write a story about the bumblebee that came into our class, and you just think 'bumblebee' and draw it, not thinking about the words of the story, just thinking 'bumblebee.'" I drew a bee. "Then what happens is that you could look at that picture and no story comes to mind.

"Here's the thing. That is not how story writers go about drawing. No way! Story writers first picture *the whole story*— they think about *what* happens first, then next, then next. They also think about details about *who* is in the story, and *where* the story takes place." I pointed to the bullets on our chart as I reminded the children of this.

How to Write a True Story

- Think of something that happened or that you did.
- Tell what happened with pictures and words.
  - Tell **who** is in the story.
  - Tell **where** the story takes place.
  - Tell **what** is happening.
- Practice telling the story in a storyteller's voice.
- Use speech bubbles to remember what people said.

Taking a class story, demonstrate how you draw the start of the story, generating words to accompany your mental image.

"Now, do you remember when that bumblebee flew right into our room last week? Do you remember that? If you want to draw that story, first thing you have to think about is how it started, who was in the story, where it took place, and what was happening. Let's do that." I closed my eyes.

"Then, I need to make drawings on the page show the reader what I saw when I remembered the start of my story. As I get ready to draw, I want to be thinking about three things: the characters (the bee, in this case), the place or the setting, and what happened. I want to be sure to draw those three things into my picture. As I draw, notice that I say the story to myself, writing-in-the-air."

I quickly drew the class on the rug under the open window with a bumblebee flying inside and dictated aloud to myself, as I drew: "During math, we sat on the rug. A bumblebee flew in the window."

Debrief, noting the transferable actions you took that you hope children also do.

"Did you guys see how I did that?" I held up a finger as I named each of the next three steps. "I thought about the first part of my story and pictured it in my mind. I pictured the people, the place, and the action. Then as I drew, I *said the words of my story out loud* to myself. Here, let me show you this chart I made that shows all those steps I took."

ACTIVE ENGAGEMENT

Rally your students to try the steps with a partner, working to draw on the wipe-off board and to say the next portion of the shared story.

"Now it is your turn. Take a second and remember what happened next in our story. Close your eyes and picture it in your mind. After the bee came in the window, what comes next? Picture *who* is in the story, *where* it takes place, and *what* happened. When you are ready, draw page two of the story on your boards and *say the words to yourself as you draw*. Go."

FIG. 3–1   My Bumblebee Story

As the children worked, I moved among them to watch and listen to their version of the second page of our story. Aiden drew only a bee and then looked at me. "How does this page go?" I asked. He said, "The bee flew at us and we were scared." I repeated what he told me and then I said, "You need to add some of that to your drawing—the bee flying at us and the people were scared."

LINK

Remind children that they need to draw and talk their stories through to support their increased focus on writing more and more conventionally.

"Guys, I saw so many of you picturing the next part of the story and then drawing the people and the place and the action. The extra exciting thing was listening to you say the words of your story as you drew. As you said the words, did any of you get ideas for what you could add to the picture?

"As you go off to write today, working not on this story but on your own, remember to draw and talk through your pictures at the same time. *And* those pictures will help you when you go to put enough letters down on the page so that people can read your words."

FIG. 3–2   The bumblebee story without words.

Understanding Children's New Levels of Dependence

As I MENTIONED IN EARLIER CONFERRING WRITE-UPS, your children may seem more dependent on you than usual now, and this should not surprise you. After all, at the start of the year you essentially invited them to pretend-write (though you didn't call it that, of course), doing as best they could without worrying themselves over whether others could read their writing. Now, suddenly, it is as though you have pulled the cloak of naivety off of them, and you are asking them to face the harsh reality of life.

You are letting them know that actually, when they write a string of letters under that word, you can't read it, and that you believe that if they slow down and work harder, they'll be able to provide enough help that you can decipher their print. So no wonder they suddenly are asking, over and over, "How do you write . . . ?" and "Can you read this?" and "Is this right?"

(continues)

MID-WORKSHOP TEACHING   **Stretching to Hold Ideas and Develop Writing**

For today's mid-workshop teaching, I decided to gather students back in the meeting area. "Writers, can I have your attention? Please take a break from your writing, and join me on the rug." Once everyone was seated, I continued on. "Writers, today I want to share a strategy that writers use. It's a pretty cool strategy, because it actually came from a technique that artists use! Have you ever heard the word *sketch* before?" A few kids nodded their heads in agreement, but I could tell that many were unfamiliar with this term. "A sketch is a quick drawing that an artist does. It's not a finished piece of art. The reason why an artist sketches is just to hold an idea. So they get their idea on paper with a quick sketch, and then *later* they go back to it to fix it up, add color, add more details, and anything else they want to do to make it better.

"Now that you all are the kinds of writers that use pictures *and* words, you can try sketching your picture quickly, just to hold your idea. Then you can hurry right along to your words. And *then*, after you get your words on the paper, you can go *back* to your sketch and add some details and colors. Let me show you how I do this." I flipped to a piece of chart paper that I had prepared earlier that resembled a page from one of the booklets.

"So I've been thinking about the time when I taught a kid I know about seed helicopters. We were sitting in the grass at the park. He picked up a maple seed and asked, 'Is this a leaf?' I told him no. 'It's a seed, a seed helicopter,' I said. 'Do you want me to fly it?' He smiled as I stood up, took the seed, and let it go. It twirled like a propeller to the ground. Laughing, he yelled, 'Let's get more!' Yes, that's definitely a story I want to write. On this first page in my booklet I think I'm going to write the first part of my story, the part when we are sitting in the park and Luke picks up the maple seed. First I'll do my sketch—let's see. . . ." The students watched as I did a quick pencil sketch of Luke and me sitting in the park, holding the maple seed. As I was sketching I voiced over, "Hmm, I'm not going to worry about what color Luke's shirt is right now. I'll get the picnic blanket in there later." I wrapped up my sketch, put my pencil down, and turned back to the class.

"Did you notice how I just quickly drew enough to hold my idea for this first page? I got the important details there—Luke holding the maple seed. I left some stuff out, like the blanket we were sitting on and the soccer ball we had with us. Those just aren't important details right now. I can go back and add them later. But now, I can go right to my words! And from now on, you can do that, too! Use your pencils to sketch your ideas, quick as lightning! Then get right to your words. Then last step, you can go back and add more details and color to your pictures!" I sent them back to their writing.

You want the message to be clear in your mind. First, you will not want to say, "Spelling doesn't matter," because, of course, it does matter. After all, people write to be read, and if the spelling is impossible to decode, then readers can't decipher a text. A more focused message might be: "It is okay to work first on figuring out what you want to say and worry later about whether the spelling works or not."

For now, though, you are not even saying, "Worry first about your content," but rather, "If you take time and work at it, you can make it *much* easier for readers to read your writing." After all, you definitely do want children to use white spaces between words as they write, not as an afterthought just prior to publication. In a similar way, you want them to work a bit to hear and record the main sounds in a word, to spell the words they know in a snap correctly, to use the word wall to help them do so, and so forth.

If children seem especially reliant on you, talk to them about this. "I'm noticing that now that you are worrying about spelling so that people can read your work, you are writing a few letters, then wanting me to say they are okay. You keep coming to me, asking, 'Is this right?' You know something? You are going to have to be the ones to

check your own writing. After you write a sentence or two, you can shift from being writer to being reader, and you can reread your own writing." Note, too, that when children do reach to you for help, you can give help in ways that support their resourcefulness and make it less likely they come to you another time. If a child says, "Is this right?" you can reply, "How do you check for whether your spelling works or not?" The child will probably shrug and say, "Read it?" Nodding, you can channel the youngster to do just that and help the youngster to evaluate whether he or she was able to read the word and to make judgments for himself or herself. Then you can simply confirm them, saying something like, "Do you see that you are able to decide this on your own? You don't need to come to me for help. You can just say, 'Let me check this myself!'"

Meanwhile, help lead small groups to be more powerful word solvers. Group your youngsters based on your spelling assessment. One group can work on labeling pictures, another on hearing final as well as first sounds in words. A third group can be nudged to write two-word labels on sentences. This work is best done on pieces the children have already written. Help children revisit those pieces in order to do more writing.

Playing with My Blocks

First I was playing in the bathroom.

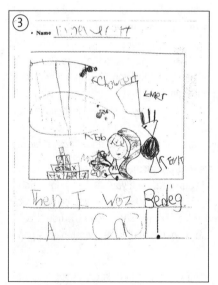

Then I was building a castle!

Finally it fell down. Then I cried.

FIG. 3–3 Tiana's block story. Tiana writes her story in the air as she draws it. She then rereads and writes the words.

Using Pictures to Help Write the Words

Celebrate that the students said the words of their story while drawing their pictures.

Writers, can you gather in the meeting area, bringing your writing from today?" Once the children had gathered, I said, "I'm glad that all of you worked hard to say the words of your story while you drew the picture. The good news is that now, you can look back at one of the story-pictures that you have drawn, and when you look at the picture, you can usually remember the story.

Point out and demonstrate that because you did the same, when you are disoriented as you write, you can refer back to your picture to remember your content.

"Let me show you how the picture can help me remember the words so I can read my writing—and so I can remember what I wanted to write, if I am only half done." I turned back to a picture I had drawn earlier of the bumblebee coming into the window. Below this picture, I'd written a few letters—an incomplete transcript of the story (which was that a bumblebee flew in the window). "I'm going to read my writing," I said, and put my finger under the words. I read "A…" but then was stymied. The letters said *Bmblebe*. "Hmmmmm. This is hard to read!" I said, silencing children who tried to chime in that this must say "bumblebee."

"Watch what I do when I can't read my words," I said, and I touched the picture. "Oh, yes, I remember! The story is: 'A bumblebee flew in the window. We looked up from the rug.' Let me try to read the words now!" I said, and this time read the words with no problem.

Recruit children to try rereading their writing, referencing their pictures if they get stuck.

"Will you try this? Go back to the first page you wrote in your own writing today. See if you can read the words. If you get stuck, try what I did. Try seeing if the picture can help. I know you thought about the words of the story while drawing the picture, so I bet they come to mind for you. Try it! Help each other, partners, if you need help."

FIG. 3–4   The words of the bumblebee story.

Writing Sentences
that Tell a Story

IN THIS SESSION, you'll teach students that writers write sentences. You'll help them transition their stories from drawings to sentences that tell their true story.

GETTING READY

✓ Student writing from prior sessions (see Connection)

✓ List of "What Makes Writing Easy to Read," generated in Session 1 (see Connection)

✓ A simple picture book, which contains a line of text underneath each picture (see Connection)

✓ Class piece of shared writing and marker (see Teaching)

✓ *Don't Let the Pigeon Drive the Bus* by Mo Willems, or other text to demonstrate speech bubbles with ending punctuation (see Mid-Workshop Teaching)

✓ Student writing folders (see Share)

COMMON CORE STATE STANDARDS: W.K.3, RL.K.1, RL.1.6, SL.K.1, L.K.1, L.K.2.a,b

---

IT IS ALWAYS CHALLENGING to plan whole-class teaching that will meet each writer where he or she is at and take that writer where he or she needs to go. But at least when you are teaching children something about the qualities or processes of effective writing, those lessons tend to be pertinent to young and old, novice and proficient writers. For example, a lesson that suggests writers make characters talk, including the exact words that a character uses, can be as relevant for a five-year-old as for a graduate student.

It is harder to teach whole-class minilessons when your focus is on the print work of writing. Whereas all writers need to work to achieve many qualities of good writing, the truth is that lessons pertaining to the print work of writing are less broadly applicable. There will be times in this unit when some of your children listen, thinking, "I already do that."

This lesson is one such time. And just as some children will think, "I already do that," there might also be a few for whom this lesson is considerably out of reach. Usually we would say that the sign that children are ready to go from writing labels to writing sentences is the fact that their labels contain more than just an initial sound. The sun is labeled *SN*, the bike, *BIK*. We are aware, then, that you could always decide to teach this as a small-group lesson. We've decided to include the minilesson because it's important that your writers are all part of a community of practice in which everyone is working like crazy to make this important leap forward. We think transparency around this goal is helpful, even though the goal will still be a bit beyond reach for some of your children. Time and again, we have found that more children are able to do this than a teacher realizes, so nudging everyone forward can produce surprising gains. And we know that children who can already write in full sentences don't always do so and, therefore, we hope this minilesson encourages them to make this a habit.

Prior to now, many of your children will have been writing one- or two-word labels alongside lots of different parts of their drawings. Now you'll help them graduate from labels to sentences. There is a lot involved in writing a sentence—the writer needs to stretch some words out, to write other words in a snap, to leave spaces between words,

---

and to use capitals and periods. Each of these tasks could conceivably become its own minilesson. This session demonstrates, instead, how all of these components work together, which is why this lesson has many underlying common core standards that contribute to its foundation. However, it is the language standards for conventions (CCSS L.K.1 and L.K.2) that will be the focus of your work today. You can be sure that each skill that is touched upon quickly in this lesson will be revisited often. The fact that you demonstrate how to do all of this together won't mean that your students can all do likewise!

"More children are able to transition from drawing to writing stories than a teacher realizes, so nudging everyone forward can produce surprising gains."

Although you'll teach something that is ambitious for some of your students—writing not just labels but whole sentences—today's session actually brings the bend-in-the-road of the unit toward a close. Tomorrow's session functions as the ending of the first portion of this unit, so there will be a celebratory feel to it. You should know from the start, however, that the second bend of this unit intensifies the focus of this first bend. Children will continue to work on writing readable true stories. The difference is that during the second bend, they'll be given charts that help them to do this work: a word wall, a rubric, a vowel chart, and the like.

This session leans on the teaching you did in the first lesson. You assume that your writers know how to stretch out words, hear more sounds, and record more letters in a word. Your writers will use these skills to help them write sentences.

Writing Sentences that Tell a Story

CONNECTION

Give the students an opportunity to generate a new anchor chart on ways to make writing easy to read and to self-assess their writing against that chart.

"Writers, come to the meeting area with your folders, and when you get here, will you take a piece of writing that you have been working on out of your folder?

"Writers, your writing muscles are really growing! Let's see our muscles!" I made a muscle in my arm, and children did the same. "You have been writing true stories—that's a challenge—*and* writing true stories that are easy to read— that's an extra big challenge. It is like you have been lifting weights.

"I thought that today, maybe we should start a chart of all the things we now know writers do to make writing easy to read, and that way you can work on all those things on your own. Will you look at the writing you just pulled out of your folder, and think about some of the things you have been doing to make your writing easier to read? You can look at this list we jotted on the very first day of this unit, too, to help you remember." I quickly read the list to the class.

A teacher recently said to me, "I'm still waiting for my kindergarteners to be ready to write sentences." I was thunderstruck. You are waiting for that? I thought. A teacher shouldn't wait for children to progress—we teach them to progress. We know what the next work is for them and we support them in doing that work.

> ### What Makes Writing Hard to Read
> the letters are smushed together — girl
> not many letters — tble
>
> ### What Makes Writing Easy to Read
> Spaces ("it isn't all scrunched together") girl
> neat ("without a lot of eraser marks") clean
> a lot of letters in every word — tables
> pictures that help — sun

When you make lists with your children, remember that less is more. Long laundry lists that include everything under the sun aren't helpful. Once you've listed three or four items, be wary against adding a lot more, especially if they simply say the same thing in different words.

After reading aloud the chart, I asked, "So, keeping that stuff in mind, and looking at the story you have in your hands, what are some things you've been doing to make your writing easier to read? We can check them off on our chart, and if they are not there, we can add them." As the students shared, I found on the chart that we'd used a different way to word the same work, and therefore checked each of the already listed items.

"Let's reread our chart, and then I'd like you to look at your own writing and give a thumbs up if you've done each thing I read from our list, and a thumbs down if it's something that you need to work on, okay?" I read over the chart, one bullet at a time, giving the students a chance to reflect on the points on the chart.

Bemoan the fact that some kids wrote labels, not getting their great stories into print.

"You all are drawing and saying amazing stories, and you are working hard to make your stories easy to read. I'm noticing that sometimes your writing is just a few labels alongside pictures. That was great at the very start of the year. But you guys are growing so quickly as writers, and your writing muscles are getting stronger and stronger, so I am hoping you can begin to write sentences. If *you* can reread the words you write beside pictures, and if *others* can read those words, those labels, then you are ready to write sentences like those you see in books." I showed a picture book that contained a line of text underneath each page's picture. "Thumbs up if your muscles are big enough for this next big challenge."

❖ **Name the teaching point.**

"Today I want to teach you that a writer says a sentence in his or her mind, then writes it, writing word after word."

TEACHING

Read the pictures of your story, saying aloud the short sentences you plan to write.

"Let's work on writing sentences together, okay? Before you can write a new sentence, it helps to reread what you have already written." I pulled out our class story about the bumblebee. "It helps to reread to remember what has already been said." I opened to the first page:

> *During math, we sat on the rug.*
> *A bumblebee flew in the window.*

The class joined in as I read the words, pointing under each one. Then I turned to the second page, where we hadn't yet written any words, but did have a picture. I said, in a tucked aside, "I forgot what we want to write, but earlier we found that the picture can remind us!" I touched the picture and retrieved, as if drawing this from the picture, the story we had intended to write, "The bee flew toward us. We were scared."

FIG. 4–1

Demonstrate the whole process of saying a word, recording it, leaving a space, then saying the next word. Don't worry that many children will not totally grasp all this. This is immersion.

"Now we need to write the words on this page, and what we learned today is that we need to first say the whole sentence to ourselves—*The bee flew toward us*—then we write it."

I picked up a marker pen, said the first word—*the*—and said, "Hey, that's on our word wall! We know it in a snap!" and then I wrote on chart paper, "The."

"Then we need to add a space between the words, don't we? So, I am going to leave a little space before I start the next word, *bee*. I don't know that word in a snap, so I am going to have to stretch it out." I said "bee," bit by bit, and wrote a letter for each sound I heard.

I reread the words (*The bee*) and then worked on the next three words. When I reached the end of the sentence, I said, "That is the end of this group of words, so I need a signal that this is the end of the group. I need a period." I put a period on the page.

ACTIVE ENGAGEMENT

Ask children to help you to write each part of the next sentence, getting them to say aloud to a partner what they write next, then recruiting some help, working on the shared story, and moving them to the next portion of the sentence.

"Can you guys help with our next sentence?" I touched the picture, as if using it to resurrect the memory of the text we wanted to write. I dictated, 'We were scared.'

"Will you tell the person beside you what we write first?" The children talked for a second, and then one hand shot up. I brought Dante up to the front of the room, and as I gave him the marker, I said, "Will it be a capital letter or lowercase?"

Taking the marker pen, Dante said, "Capital?"

I nodded. "It is the start of another sentence, so you need a line leader."

After Dante wrote *We*, I asked children to tell their partners what they would do or write next. Overhearing the children, I pointed right beside the last letter of *we*. "Do we write here?" I asked, and in that way, elicited that we needed to leave a space between words. Dante, with help from the class, wrote *wer* for *were*. When we reached the word *scared*, I again asked children to say the word slowly, listening to sounds. I called on them for suggestions, writing just the dominant sounds. At the end of the line, I put a period, without a lot of discussion.

FIG. 4–2

If your progress through the sentence feels too slow or you begin to lose children's focused attention, you can always say, "Let's stop there, and some of you can help me finish this page later."

Notice the number of decisions that are involved in writing a three-word-long sentence! Writing is no easy task for novices!

LINK

Remind writers to write sentences using what they learned about capital letters, spaces, and periods whenever they are working to make writing that is easy to read.

"Guys, you are amazing at this big work! So, I want you to remember after this that whenever you write, you can say the words of your story and then write them, one by one. As you go to write the words on the lines below your picture, you will remember all that you know about writing words. Don't forget to put a capital letter at the start of a sentence and a period at the end."

FIG. 4–3

Support Students as They Shift from Writing Labels to Writing Sentences

ALTHOUGH YOU HAVE TAUGHT A MINILESSON that encourages children to shift from writing labels to writing sentences underneath their picture, the truth is that this instruction is best done through one-to-one conferences. In an ideal world, you'll be able to work with each individual just as he or she is on the cusp of going from writing labels to writing sentences so that you can provide the support to make sure this transition works well. But that won't happen. Before this minilesson, and after it, you will have children who embark on writing sentences without help from you, and as a result, it is predictable that many of them will produce what looks like random strings of letters. Think about it: When writing a label beside each of a dozen pictures, the child didn't need to worry about segmenting her words. She could write *bik* beside the bike, and *sistr* beside the sister. But if she is writing, *My sister rode my bike*, then all of a sudden, the writer needs to figure out how to differentiate one word from the next.

Because children will be apt to produce writing that is unreadable to them and to you, both, it is important to watch writers in the act of writing a sentence that they have just articulated out loud. For example, after Juliser approached me with her writing many times over the last few days, asking each time, "Can you read this?" and learning that more often than not, neither Juliser nor I could read her little text, I decided it was time to help her *during* the act of composition. I already knew that many of her oral stories were often filled with details about the adventures she and her mother had together. I pulled up a chair next to her, and watched her work, leaning low into her paper, saying a string of sounds out loud, writing letter after letter in an unbroken line. It was as if her voice pushed letters out onto the page: "Itikwmimomeinrk."

I intervened. "Juliser, may I stop you?" Waiting for her eyes, I then pressed on. "Juliser, I am going to ask you the question we have been asking each other a lot over the last few days. Can you read this?"

Juliser began, "I took my mommy . . ." Her voice trailed off. She looked to me with the beginning swimmer look. As soon as she gave me that look, I jumped right in with her. "Juliser, what was this page supposed to say? When you said your story, what did it

MID-WORKSHOP TEACHING
Using Ending Punctuation in Speech Bubbles

"Writers, I'm going to interrupt your work for just one minute. I want to show you something really cool! Can you all join me in the meeting area, please?" I waited until the students had assembled on the rug. "Look at this! Look at what Mo Willems did in *Don't Let the Pigeon Drive the Bus*! He writes just like you do!" I held the book open and drew attention to the speech bubbles. "Whenever the pigeon says anything, Mo uses speech bubbles to show that he's talking, see! Just like you guys do in *your* writing.

"Can I tell you something else that Mo does? Something that you can do in your writing, too?" The students leaned in closer, eager to be let in on a new writing secret. "Not only does Mo use speech bubbles to let his readers know that the pigeon is talking, but he uses special punctuation, like exclamation points and question marks, to let his readers know just *how* the pigeon is talking. Let me show you." I turned to a page where the pigeon was asking a question and read a bit. "See on this page? The speech bubble says 'Please?' That question mark at the end of the sentence helps readers know that the pigeon is *asking* to drive the bus. We know that he's pretty much begging, right? And let me show you another very cool punctuation mark, the exclamation point." I flipped to a page with an exclamation point and read. "On this page, the pigeon says 'C'mon! Just once around the block!' And because those sentences have exclamation points at the end of them, I know to read in a very excited voice, because the pigeon is very enthusiastic. That's what the exclamation point tells me.

"So writers, I'm going to send you back to your writing. And now you have another tool for your writing backpack. Not only can you use speech bubbles in your writing to show that someone is talking, but you can use ending punctuation like question marks and exclamation points to show just *how* they are talking." I sent the students back to their work.

say?" Juliser looked down at her picture, then back up at me. "It was about me and my mommy went bike riding in the park."

I repeated back to Juliser what she said she wanted to write. "Okay, 'Me and my mommy went bike riding in the park.' Let's write it together. As we write, we'll go back often to the start of the sentence and read it again. Okay?" Juliser nodded in agreement.

"Juliser, say the sentence that you want to write. Say all the words." I wanted to give Juliser a clear, brief prompt and then allow her to proceed independently.

"Me and my mommy went bike riding in the park."

"Alright, let's start with the first word. Say the first word."

"Me," Juliser said.

I prompted her, "Say that word again. What is the first sound that you hear?" Juliser said it again.

"/Mmmm/."

"Good, write the letter that makes that sound." She did. "Okay, now read that." As I spoke, I put Juliser's finger under the letter she had just written.

"/Mm/."

"What else do you hear in that word?" I asked, directing Juliser's finger so that it now pointed to the empty space beside the letter she'd written.

"I hear /eeeee/."

"Good. Now write the letter that makes that sound." As Juliser finished recording the e, I continued, "Excellent! Now read that."

Juliser responded, "Me."

"Are those the only sounds you hear?" She nodded her head. "Okay, so it looks like we've come to the end of the word. Reread what you have written so far, again. Remember we said we would reread often?"

I took Juliser's finger and again put it under the first letter. Juliser read, "Me."

"Now let me see if I can reread it." I put my finger under the word and voiced "/mm/" and then proceeded to the e. "I can read it!" I said. "Yippee!"

I pressed on, but now let the intervals between my prompts become longer, so that Juliser could become accustomed to doing this work with less support from me. "Let's keep going, okay?" I continued. "We need to leave a blank space because we are at the end of a word. It is as if the paper needs a rest before a new word starts. Now, what word comes next?"

"And," said Juliser. "Hey, wait! I know that word—it's on our word wall. A-n-d." She quickly wrote that word on her paper, and I again reminded her to leave a blank space afterward and then reread all that she had written so far. Juliser did, and then we continued on together, Juliser writing mommy and went. All the while I sat by her side but offered her less and less support. It was time for me to move on, but I wanted to make sure that before I left, I named for her what she had done as a writer and left her with a reminder to continue this work in the future.

"Juliser, I know it feels like we are rereading a lot of times to get this page of the story written, but it is really important for you to keep rereading often as you write the rest of this page and the rest of your story. Remember that I will be sitting at home tonight trying to read your writing, but you won't be there to help me. You need to help me now by the way you do this writing, okay? What will your next word be?" Before I moved on, Juliser said, "Bike," had written a b, and was rereading it.

"Remember, as you are writing words into sentences, you will come to some words that you don't have to stretch. When Omar was writing his sentence, he realized that he was stretching every word—even words that he knew really well! It was as if he got stuck, stretching words. He was stuck in must-stretch, must-stretch, must-stretch mode," I said in my best hypnotized zombie voice. "So, pay attention to yourself and be careful not to get stuck stretching words you already know how to spell."

It is important to point out that although Juliser had been struggling to write readable writing, she was actually ready to make the step ahead to writing sentences. Some children may not be. You can still invite those children to approximate writing, producing strings of letters where the sentences in a story traditionally are written, but the important thing will be to make sure that children who are not yet writing with initial and final sounds in a word (correct ones, or approximate ones) are channeled to continue writing tons and tons of labels, even as they may or may not also leapfrog ahead to making sentence-like approximations.

These novice writers will need help writing labels in which they record at least the first and last sounds in a word. You can teach these writers to say the word slowly, then to return to just the start of the word and say the first sound. The choice of letters need not be perfect—aim to support children doing this with independence, even at the cost of accuracy. Expect children to use the letter names, not letter sounds, so the "dog" may be labeled with a *W*, which is a wise choice if one is listening to the name, not the sound made by the letter. If a child doesn't know sound-letter correspondence, channel the child to look at a chart of class names for help. "*P* like Peter!" the child will say. Children who are writing labels can add a second word to the label, writing "my dog" instead of "dog," and in that way, get some practice leaving spaces between words and using high-frequency words (from the word wall) in combination with words that need to be sounded out.

The most important thing to say about children who struggle to hear beginning and ending sounds and who, therefore, continue to label, is that these children need lots of practice saying words slowly and listening for and isolating sounds. Be sure they are labeling half a dozen things on a page, not just one! Make sure they write a label, then reread it, checking that they have recorded the sounds, changing what they have written if need be. And remember that even if you are not near the child and if the resulting label is nothing you can read, it is still important for the child to have lots of practice saying words slowly, listening for sounds, and doing the best he or she can to record those sounds.

FIG. 4-4

Writing Sentences

Bring some writers who are strong at writing sentences into a fishbowl and name the process those writers use.

"Guys, I have some of our writers in the middle of the rug, and I asked them to continue to write sentences while we watch. I want each of you to watch the writer that is easiest for you to see. We are going to notice all that he or she does to write in groups of words, in sentences." (See Figures 4–5 and 4–6.)

The writers began to write, and the rest of the class watched the writer closest to them. I moved among the writers, naming the work they were doing as they did it. After a minute or two, while the writers continued working, I asked the observers to talk to the person next to them about what they noticed. As they talked, the writers worked.

Then I dismissed the fishbowl and asked the whole class to discuss what they had seen. Lilly said, "I saw Kayla start with a small letter and then fix it because it was the first one." "In a sentence?" I added. Lilly nodded. I nodded.

① I took a bath. My mom put bubbles in the water. I felt good.

② I put toys in the bath. I looked in the water for the Lego man.

③ I found it. I splashed in the water. I got clean.

FIG. 4–5   Kayla's bath story

"Are we going to the park?" "Yes, Sheena."

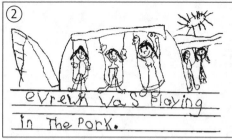

Everyone was playing in the park.

"Let's go home."

FIG. 4–6   Sheena's park story

Joey added, "I saw Sheena use her finger to check if there was enough space between words." And, finally Kyla piped in with, "They were reading it, like after, after they put it down, they did the rereading."

"Good noticing, guys. Capital letters and spaces and a lot of rereading are all important when writing sentences. I know your stories will be so much easier to read as you make these things part of your writing. Would you, right now, reread the story you worked on today, and check that you are including everything on the 'What Makes Writing Easy to Read' list. As you do that, I will add today's new things to our list."

> ### What Makes Writing Easy to Read
> Spaces ("it isn't all scrunched together") girl
> neat ("without a lot of eraser marks") clean
> pictures that help   sun
> hear lots of sounds in a word   ka ch
> leave spaces between words   I walked my dog.
> make pictures that hold the words of the
> story   Love
> Use CAPITALS at the start of a sentence
> Use punctuation at the end of a sentence.
> . ! ? , . ! ?

The Power of Rereading

DURING THIS LAST SESSION in the first bend, you will be shining a spotlight on one of the most important behaviors for a kindergarten writer. In the unit so far you have been working with your writers to make sure that they are using pictures to help them imagine language and to help them hold onto meaning. You have been teaching them how to write in groups of words with spaces and capitals and periods. Your writers are probably deeply engaged in the work of writing easy-to-read true stories.

When you look around your workshop, you might see kids bent over their papers with a serious look on their faces. This unit asks your writers to bring a level of focus to their work that is demanding. Rereading can help make sure that this demanding work is also rewarding. When beginners are concentrating so hard on so many new things, they are in danger of losing their way, and rereading can help them find their way over and over again.

You will want to make sure that you demonstrate rereading on many different levels. Writers reread a word over and over as they listen for more sounds and add more letters. Writers reread words over and over as they work on the group of words that is a sentence. And writers reread whole pages to make sure that what they wrote looks right, sounds right, and makes sense. When they do all of these kinds of rereading on a consistent basis, your kindergartners will be well on their way to making writing that is so much easier to read. Meanwhile, they'll also be on the way to becoming conventional readers as well.

It's helpful to make this enticing and fun for children by suggesting they think of their pencils as tools for both writing and rereading. To teach this, you will show them that just as they can flip their pencil back and forth from its writing side to its reading side, they need to flip their brains back and forth from the writing side to the reading side. Writing that is easy to read is made by writers who switch from writer to reader and back again.

IN THIS SESSION, you'll teach students that for a variety of reasons, writers reread often. They write a little and then read a little, flipping back and forth between being a writer and a reader.

GETTING READY

- ✔ Chart paper, markers (see Connection)

- ✔ Pencils with erasers, one for each student (see Teaching and Active Engagement)

- ✔ Class piece of shared writing, with pictures and words on pages 1–2, and just pictures on page 3 (see Teaching)

- ✔ List of "What Makes Writing Easy to Read" (see Link)

COMMON CORE STATE STANDARDS: W.K.3, W.K.5, RFS.K.1, SL.K.1, L.K.1, L.K.2

The Power of Rereading

CONNECTION

Celebrate the hard work children have been doing as they work to make their writing readable, and point out that sometimes the focus on words disorients a writer, leading the writer to forget the overall content.

"Writers, when I watched you write yesterday, I was amazed by your focus! It was actually hard to see your faces because at every table, your heads were bent low over papers as you worked to make your true stories easier to read. Leo even looked up at me and said, 'Whew! This is really hard work!' He looked happy about his hard work. I think he is discovering what you are all discovering, that making writing in ways that other people can *really read* is the most amazing thing to do.

"As I watched you yesterday, I realized that because you were all concentrating so hard on making each word readable, some of you forgot the story. We talked earlier about how it can help, in those times when you forget what you are trying to say, to look back at the picture and to use it to help remember the story. Today I want to teach you another thing that writers do to hold onto the whole big story."

❖ **Name the teaching point.**

"Here is my tip: writers reread—often, for lots of reasons. Writers write a little, and then read a little, flipping back and forth between being writer and reader of the story."

TEACHING

Suggest that pencils can be magic because one end is good for writing, the other for tapping at words as one rereads.

"You know, guys, when I do the work of a writer, sometimes I think of pencils as magic. The pencil can be a tool for switching between writing and rereading because you can flip it to one side," I flipped to the lead point, "and write, and to the other side," I flipped to the eraser and tapped the words, "and reread. The pencil has a writing side and a reading side."

It is tradition to start a minilesson by reviewing what children did previously, but usually a teacher recalls his or her teaching. This focus on the work children did on the preceding day is a nice alternative.

Today's minilesson fits, in a way, with a few other sessions that all combine to provide writers with a collection of strategies for recalling the story they want to write. So there are some reasons for making a chart to accompany today's minilesson, putting today's strategy alongside other possible strategies for accomplishing the job. In the end, because there are already two charts threading through the unit, we voted against this chart, but you can decide based on your own students. Such a chart could look like this:

> *How a Writer Remembers the Whole Story*
> * *Writers think of the story when making the picture.*
> * *Writers tell and retell a story across their fingers.*
> * *Writers look back at the picture when they are stuck.*
> * *Writers reread often.*

I held up my pencil as I said, "I started thinking about your pencil as this magic tool for switching between writing and rereading when I was working with Darien yesterday. He was working on a page of his story, and he worked like this—watch!" Role-playing Darien, I flipped my pencil from the point side, whereupon I wrote a few letters, to the eraser side, whereupon I reread what I wrote, tapping under the word. "Darien did this flip every time he needed to go from putting letters on the page to reading what he wrote. He used his pencil as a tool to help him reread. And there are so so *so* many reasons to reread when you are writing!"

Demonstrate the shifts between writing and rereading as you continue to work on the class story.

"Let's go back and work through our story. Watch how many times we read—using this end of our pencil—and write—using that end.

"Okay, what does our story say anyway? Hmmm." I left a tiny space in which I hoped children realized that one way to start recalling a story is to read the picture. I then acted as if I'd just recalled this and ran the eraser end of my pencil lightly around on the first page of the bumblebee booklet. I said, "Let's use the picture to help us remember the story we wanted to tell on these pages. Remember that we wanted to write about how a bumblebee flew in the window and right at us when we were on the rug?" Then, in an aside, I noted, "Do you see how the eraser end of the pencil can help us reread our picture to remember how our story goes?"

Still keeping the eraser end of my pencil down, I said, "Now we need to reread what we already wrote on this page." I pointed under each word as I read, "'A bumblebee flew in the window. We looked up from the rug.' Again, we reread with this side of my pencil to help us remember the words we wrote so far on this page." I modeled this technique again, this time reading the words on the second page. "'The bee flew toward us. We were scared.'

"Now it's time to switch to writer," I said, flipping my pencil over to the point side. "Let's go to the third page in our bumblebee story. We've already done our picture, but we have no words. So let's go back to that picture and use it to help us tell the story we wanted to say." I flipped my pencil around to the eraser side and moved it lightly around the picture as I thought out loud. "That's right, the bee went above our heads and landed right on the chart paper." There were a few chuckles from the class as the students recalled this incident. "Okay, so we want to write 'The bee went above our heads.' I know the first word, *The*, so I can write it quickly!" I flipped my pencil back to the writing side and wrote *The* on my paper. "The next word in my sentence is *bee*. I need to stretch that word." I flipped my pencil to the eraser side and moved it a little from left to right as I listened for the sounds in the word *bee*. I said, "The eraser side can help me pay attention to the sounds in a word before I try to match the sounds to the letters."

I wrote the letters *b-e* and then quickly flipped my pencil to the eraser side and reread the first two words of my sentence. "Did you see how once I had worked hard to stretch the word *bee*, I really needed to reread what I had written so far to help me go forward and write the next word?"

Debrief in ways that highlight the work you hope students will transfer to their own writing.

"That's what writers do. They are both writers and readers of their writing, and their pencil can help them do this switching. Writers can use rereading of a word to help them hear more sounds and add more letters. They can use rereading of

Notice that this minilesson revisits a concept that you have emphasized repeatedly. So although the notion that pencils are magic, containing a writing and a reading side, is new, the larger point is one that threads through this unit.

This is detailed, sequential work. It needs to be taught in this very procedural step-by-step way because this minilesson offers a how-to text, and the steps are easy to jumble together, to bypass. The flip of the pencil helps accentuate the metacognitive work kids are required to do as they problem solve their way through the hard work of spelling, putting readable words on the page.

FIG. 5–1

some words in a sentence to help them remember the rest of the words in a sentence. Writers can also reread whole sentences to make sure their groups of words tell the story the writer wanted to tell."

ACTIVE ENGAGEMENT

Channel students to do some pretend writing with pretend magic pencils, where they again shift back and forth between writing and rereading.

"Now it's your turn. I want you guys to hold your pencils as if you are doing the writing of the rest of this sentence. You are going to be pretend-writing. You will actually write in the air. Don't forget the magic power in both ends of your pencil. As it flips, so do you, from writer to reader and back again."

The children held their pencils in the air as if poised over imaginary paper. I said, "Let's reread what we have written so far in the sentence we started." All of the kids flipped their pencils to the eraser end. We all pointed under the words—*The bee*—as we reread them.

With his eraser down, Simon said, "Next we need to write *went*." I nodded and made a very dramatic flip from one end of the pencil to the other.

"Wait, wait," Chloe added. "We could use the reading side when we are writing *went* to help us hear sounds." She said, "went," and with her eraser, she swept her pretend pencil in front of her.

"Good," I said, and did the same on chart paper. "Finish this sentence on your own pretend paper. Think about what happened on this page, and say the word, listening for sounds. After you write *The bee went* you can finish the sentence—*The bee went above our heads*. and I will do the same thing."

The children wrote in the air, and their pencils flipped. Like magic wands or music batons their pencils pretend-recorded the words of the sentence in a rhythm of writing and rereading. Meanwhile, I finished writing our story together, using the same procedures.

page 1 A bumblebee flew in the window. We looked up from the rug.

page 2 The bee flew toward us. We were scared.

page 3 The bee went above our heads and landed right on the chart paper.

FIG. 5–2

Debrief by celebrating the kids' engagement as they shifted between pretend writing and pretend reading, flipping pencils between the writing end (the lead) and the reading end (the eraser).

"You guys, that was so beautiful. I saw all of you using your pencils for writing *and* for rereading. None of you had that lost look on your face. You knew that if your writing pencil got stuck, you could switch to your reading pencil and that would help you find your way again."

LINK

Recall the teaching point, and then send writers off to work.

"Writers, today is the last day in this bend in the road of our unit. It is sort of like an ending to Chapter 1 in the unit, *Writing Stories that People Can Really* Read. I'm not going to tell you about the new ways in which you will work starting in your next writing workshop—but it will be a bit new.

"So today needs to be a celebration of all you have learned about making your writing easy to read. You'll have a chance to write one more true story today, unless you are in the middle of a story you started yesterday. Right now, can you think of what this last special story will be about—something you did, something that happened to you?" I left a moment of silence. "I can tell most of you have ideas for the story you will write today.

"Here is the thing. Today, will you use all your muscles to make your writing as easy to read as is possible? I'm going to read off the things you have been taught to do, and each time I read something, if you think you have the strength to do that in today's story, show me your muscles." I read the list, allowing time for a show of strength between each item and adding one last item from today's minilesson to the list.

There have been lots of times when the teacher rereads a chart full of tips, asking children to note which of the items they can do, or have done. This ritual is kept vital and alive because the actual lists change, and because the accompanying actions change. "If you have the strength to do that . . . show me your muscles" is a new one—and has got to be an all-time favorite! Consider the life lessons in that invitation!

> What Makes Writing Easy to Read
> Spaces ("it isn't all scrunched together") girl
> neat ("without a lot of eraser marks") clean
> pictures that help   sun ☼
> hear lots of sounds in a word   (xo) (ch)
> leave spaces between words   I walked my dog.
> make pictures that hold the words of the
> story ♡ Love
> Use   CAPITALS at the start of a sentence
> Use punctuation at the end of a sentence.
>   .!?,.!?

"So you've said you can do these things. Now, superhero muscle-people, show me! Off you go."

Asking Questions to Foster Independence and Possibility for Writers

ONE OF OUR BIGGEST GOALS in writing workshop is to encourage young writers to develop their own independence and sense of possibility for their own writing. In his book *Choice Words*, Peter Johnston believes this vision for the student is crucial, but equally important is the teacher's ability to "view the present child as competent and on that basis imagine new possibilities" (2004, 29, citing A. Haas Dyson, *Research in the Teaching English*, May 1999). Every session in this unit is born from that type of teacher belief in the ability of kindergarten students. It is our job to teach children the skills and strategies that will help them believe that they can totally do this work! We do this by not only raising the bar of possibility but also by creating a narrative for students about who they are as writers.

Johnston says that those stories "shape who we think we are," and underneath this narrative, we need to foster that sense of perseverance. As Johnston further notes, "To solve the many problems I will encounter as a writer, and to persist through the many revisions I will face, I have to weave myself into a narrative in which I am the kind of person who encounters and solves problems with texts" (2004, 20). Of course, this kind of work happens in all parts of our lesson, but it can be particularly effective in our conferring and small-group work. It is this philosophy that will guide all of our work with writers.

In our conversations with children about their writing, Johnston offers us some questions that we can use to affect teaching that is about both strategy and agency. More elaboration for these questions can be found in Johnston's book, but here are some of his core questions that focus on both problem solving and possibility:

> How did you figure that out? (31)
>
> What problems did you come across today? and then, What can you do? (adapted from Becoming Literate, Marie Clay, 1991, 32)
>
> How are you planning to go about this? (33)
>
> Where are you going with this piece of writing? (33)

MID-WORKSHOP TEACHING
Rereading Writing to Make Sure It Is Easy to Read

"Writers, can you look up for a second? You know today will be a celebration of sorts. We're going to put today's story out on display for all the kids to read. At the end of today, everyone will take their magic pencils and flip to the reading side, and with those reading pencils, all of you will go from desk to desk, reading each other's writing—*if you can.*

"So you just have a bit more time to finish today's writing and to make sure that you have used the items on our chart to make your writing as readable as it can be. The very last thing on the chart is especially important—you will want to reread your writing often because if *you* can't reread it, others won't be able to either.

"Would you all flip your pencils over to the rereading side and do some re-reading right now to make sure that your stories are easy to read? Remember, if you find something that needs to be fixed, switch back to the writing side of your pencil and fix it. I am going to set the timer for two minutes for you to reread for that time. When the bell rings, you can go back to the writing work I interrupted. Remember that you need to finish today's writing so you can share it with the class."

> Which part are you sure about and which part are you not sure about? (34)

As you make your way through the rest of the teaching in this unit, you will probably want to try sprinkling these questions into your conferring and small-group work with students.

Celebrating Readable Stories

Celebrate the hard work of writing readable stories by having a Readable True Stories Museum.

Ask students to put their finished stories on top of their desks and come to the rug with their magic pencils. "Writers, I am so excited to celebrate our writing today. We are going to have a Readable True Stories Museum. Are you ready for that? Just like when you go to an art museum and walk around admiring all of the beautiful art, in our Readable True Stories Museum you will stroll around and admire all of the wonderfully written true stories. You will need your magic pencils, flipped to the reading side. Does everyone have their magic pencils? Good. Before we head out to the museum, let's take a quick look at our chart so that we're reminded of all the ways that we have been working to make our stories easier to read.

"For the next few minutes, you'll each take a walk through our museum. Be sure to stop often, and read lots of writing. You have all been working so hard to make your writing readable, now is the time to celebrate! Happy reading!"

I was skateboarding in the rain and I was going to the train station.

I went to the store to buy my hat.

I saw my grandmother.

FIG. 5–1   Brian's skateboarding story

Checklists Can Help Writers Make Powerful Stories

IN THIS SESSION, you'll teach students that writers use tools, such as checklists, to help them write the best they can.

GETTING READY

- Student writing folders containing writing from the entire unit, including the piece that was celebrated in the Session 5 celebration (see Connection)

- Photographs or pictures of people doing something that is made easier with the assistance of a tool, which could include bulldozers, levers, wheelbarrows, or even blenders for chefs (see Connection)

- Enlarged copy of the Narrative Writing Checklist, Grades K and 1, covered with a cloth so that it can be revealed with a flourish (see Teaching) 🌸

- Teacher-created writing sample to model using the Narrative Writing Checklist, as well as revised writing sample to reflect use of the checklist (see Teaching and Share)

- List of "What Makes Writing Easy to Read" (see Link)

- Student writing sample that models using the Narrative Writing Checklist, Grades K and 1 to improve the writing (see Mid-Workshop Teaching)

COMMON CORE STATE STANDARDS: W.K.3, W.K.5, W.K.6, W.1.3, RL.K.1, RL.K.2.b, RL.K.3, SL.K.1, L.K.1.f, L.K.2

HOPEFULLY YOU WILL HAVE HAD A CHANCE to read over children's writing, noting ways in which it has and has not improved since the start of the unit and of the year. Chances are good that the writing has already become more conventional and easier to read. This should be a source of real pleasure for you because every bit of progress your children make as writers will give them important traction in their reading as well. When Marie Clay, the great reading researcher who founded Reading Recovery, visited Teachers College Reading and Writing classes, she told us her one biggest regret about her program, Reading Recovery, was that she hadn't named it Reading *and Writing* Recovery and made a bigger point about the central role that writing plays in supporting young readers. Clay told us that in her eyes, a child is ready to read conventionally—to move into level C books—if the child can write in a way that he or she can reread the writing and an adult can reread at least swatches of the writing, doing so with one-to-one matching. This unit is taking children a long way toward writing and reading with that level of proficiency.

But progress sometimes comes with a cost, and it is likely that you have noticed that although your children's writing is more conventional, it may also be less fluent, less detailed, less expressive, and less coherent. This shouldn't surprise you. Throughout the year, you'll find that when you emphasize a new aspect of writing (as you will have done with your new emphasis on conventions), some children will forget all your prior instruction. In this instance, children will be especially prone to forget concerns over content because a focus on convention not only is different from a focus on content but it also conflicts with a focus on content. This is why we, as adult writers, often say, when we are drafting, "I'll just spell as best I can for now and come back later to fix it." Of course, a concern for convention will be all the more taxing on a young child, for whom very little has reached the level of automaticity. And so it shouldn't surprise you if your children have focused less on their content and craft now that your teaching has created a new concern for mechanics.

This session, then, is one of several during this unit that spotlights not the importance of writing so that readers can read the text, but instead, writing well-developed stories in the first place. Like the earlier sessions that focused on narrative craft, this session essentially asks children to remember all they know about writing stories, to extend that knowledge just a bit, and to draw on what they know as they write. The features of narrative writing that are highlighted are essential ones, and the goal is not perfection but progress. Through this exercise we extend our work with the Common Core writing standard, which asks students to order events and provide a reaction (W.K.3) by also asking them to consider character and setting details underscored in the standards for Reading Literature (RL.K.1, RL.K.2, and RL.K.3) and incorporate them into their story. We also set students well on a path for achieving the grade 1 writing standards, which, in addition to the grade K standards, expect students to recount two or more events and provide a sense of closure (W.1.3).

"The goal of narrative writing is not perfection but progress."

The checklist that you uncover and use in this session is part of an entire assessment system that undergirds not only this book but this series of books. You will see this list resurface later in this unit with grade 1 expectations alongside kindergarden expectations, and many or most of your children will reach grade 1 expectations before this year is over. We recomment this—the CCSS escalates rapidly in middle school, and we aim to send students to those grades doing work that is highly proficient (that is, for kindergarteners, meeting first-grade standards). During the units on narrative writing, the different versions of the checklist will undergird instruction and assessment.

Checklists Can Help Writers Make Powerful Stories

CONNECTION

Orient children to the start of a new bend in the unit, helping them know they'll continue to write readable true stories, this time using new tools.

"Writers, when you come to our meeting area, bring your folders and get out the story that you celebrated in the museum during our last writing workshop." They did this. "Writers, I know you remember the celebration you had during our last writing workshop. That celebration marked the ending of the first part of this unit. Today, then, starts some new work.

"The work won't be *all* new. You will still write true stories every day during writing time, and you will still write in booklets. You will still think about things that happen to you, and tap the pages of your book, then tell the story that goes on each page, then sketch and write it. You will still write sentences, and you will still use the chart to make your writing easy to read.

"But in one important way, your work will be a bit different. Look at these pictures and tell me if you notice something about the way that all these people are working," I said, "because that will give you a hint about how your writing work will be a bit different over the next stretch of time." I showed children a small collection of pictures, each featuring someone doing some heavy lifting work that was made easier because of the use of a tool: a shovel, an electric saw, a bulldozer, and a blender.

The children noticed that the workers all used tools, and I nodded. "During this next bend in the road of the unit, you won't rely on just your bare hands to make your writing readable—you'll have the help of tools. These won't be power saws, and bulldozers, or blenders. Instead, they will be the tools that writers use."

❖ **Name the teaching point.**

"Today I want to teach you that writers use tools to help them write the best that they can. One of the tools that help writers write powerful true stories is a checklist. This may seem like a simple thing, but writers know that checklists can help them make their writing the best it can be."

TEACHING

Tell children about a time when checklists have proven very valuable.

"Writers, let me tell you a story. A few years ago, a pilot was flying an airplane, and all of a sudden he realized something was broken on that plane. It wasn't working. He thought, 'Oh no, this plane is broken. And I have hundreds of people on board.' For a second he was really worried. Then he remembered. 'Wait, I have a checklist that tells me the things to do when a plane is broken.' And quick as a wink, he pulled out that checklist—while the plane was starting to go down—and he did the first thing on the list, then the next, the next, and pretty soon this man landed the plane, safe as can be, on the Hudson River. Then he helped the people climb out and stand on the giant wings of the plane until motor boats came and picked them up.

"Everyone called the pilot a hero because most people would have been so scared; they would not have done every single thing right and brought the plane to safety. But the pilot said, 'I am not a hero. This checklist is the hero. All I did was follow the items, one by one.'

"There are whole books for grown-ups that came from that story because grown-ups started to realize that a checklist does not look like a fancy tool, but actually it is. Because the list reminds people to do all the things that the most experienced people in the world have decided really matter."

Tell children that all writers across their school will have checklists to remind them of the things writers do to make a good story and to make other kinds of writing good writing, too.

"So today, I want to tell you that in this school, all the kids—kindergartners, first-graders, even fifth-graders—will be given checklists that writers can follow (like that pilot followed the checklist for saving the plane) that will make your writing as good as it can be. And writers will get one checklist if they are writing stories and a different checklist if they are making other kinds of writing. The checklist we'll be using is for stories, for narratives, and you've seen it during the first unit. That's how it's supposed to be—you pull out the checklist often to see if you are doing more things on the list."

With a flourish, reveal part of the checklist for kindergartners, and remind children how it is used, using it to assess an imaginary and problematic piece by an unknown child.

"Are you ready?" With a great flourish, I pulled away a cloth that had been draped over an enlarged version of the checklist, displayed on the easel.

"Like we did in our last unit, I'll read an item from the checklist, and then you read over the writing you celebrated already and think, 'What can I do to make this more true?' Talk over your plans with your partner."

I read the first three skills aloud, one by one, and let children talk about it before moving on to the next item.

"Let's take a look at this piece of writing, done by my friend Rufus." I held a piece of writing in the air. "I'll read his piece over. We know that Rufus wrote, drew, and told a story, so let's think about the next point on our checklist: My story has a page that showed what happened first. Will you help me to decide whether it already matches the checklist, or would he need to make some changes?" I read the piece:

> I like rabbits. I like all colors of rabbits. I like babies and mommies and mommies with babies. I have a rabbit except he died.

"What do you think? Did Rufus tell what happened first?" I left just a tiny space for children to say no (or yes, mistakenly) and then answered my own question. "I don't think so. So writers, just like the pilot's checklist told him what to do, this checklist told Rufus what to do so he wrote his book *again*—and this time he told what happened first. He told what happened first, then next, then next. And he also put his pages in order, the next point on the checklist. Now Rufus has a new book about his rabbit and it goes like this:

> It was snowy. I fed my rabbit. He is brown. He did not wake up.

> I touched him and he was dead.

"Let's look at one more item on the checklist: 'My story indicated who was there, what they did, and how the characters felt.'

"Does Rufus tell details about the characters? Remember, characters are the people or animals. Let's look for evidence." I pointed to and underlined some examples in his piece and said, "I think he does."

Debrief in ways that spotlight the transferable process that you used and you hope children use as well, now and always.

"Rufus did a very smart thing as a writer. He used a checklist to help him make his writing the best that it can be. Just like a checklist was an important tool for that airplane pilot, this checklist was also a very important writing tool for Rufus. Using the checklist, he was able to figure out what was a little 'thumbs down' about his writing and then fix it to make it all 'thumbs up.'"

Notice that we emphasize that the checklist helps writers out because it gives writers a pathway to success, it tells writers (and specifically, Rufus) what they can do next to produce a successful piece. We are working hard to steer kids away from glancing at a piece of writing and then merrily going "check, check, check." In other checklist conversations, you'll see us emphasize that the important thing is to read the writing closely, looking for evidence. Sometimes we encourage students to annotate the piece of writing, citing where they have found evidence. The Narrative Writing Checklist can be found on the CD-ROM.

Narrative Writing Checklist

	Kindergarten	NOT YET	STARTING TO	YES!	Grade 1	NOT YET	STARTING TO	YES!
	Structure				**Structure**			
Overall	I told, drew, and wrote a whole story.	☐	☐	☐	I wrote about when I did something.	☐	☐	☐
Lead	I had a page that showed what happened first.	☐	☐	☐	I tried to make a beginning for my story.	☐	☐	☐
Transitions	I put my pages in order.	☐	☐	☐	I put my pages in order. I used words such as *and* and *then, so*.	☐	☐	☐
Ending	I had a page that showed what happened last in my story.	☐	☐	☐	I found a way to end my story.	☐	☐	☐
Organization	My story had a page for the beginning, a page for the middle, and a page for the end.	☐	☐	☐	I wrote my story across three or more pages.	☐	☐	☐
	Development				**Development**			
Elaboration	My story indicated who was there, what they did, and how the characters felt.	☐	☐	☐	I put the picture from my mind onto the page. I had details in pictures and words.	☐	☐	☐
Craft	I drew and wrote some details about what happened.	☐	☐	☐	I used labels and words to give details.	☐	☐	☐
	Language Conventions				**Language Conventions**			
Spelling	I could read my writing.	☐	☐	☐	I used all I knew about words and chunks of words (*at, op, it*, etc.) to help me spell.	☐	☐	☐
	I wrote a letter for the sounds I heard.	☐	☐	☐	I spelled all the word wall words right and used the word wall to help me spell other words.	☐	☐	☐
	I used the word wall to help me spell.	☐	☐	☐		☐	☐	☐

ACTIVE ENGAGEMENT

Channel children to reread and assess their own narratives in light of the same two criteria.

"Now please get your writing out, and I will reread the checklist. Then you and your partner will talk about whether the checklist tells *you* what you can do when you write your story over again. This time, you'll be looking at both the kindergarten *and* the first-grade goals. Some of you are already doing things on the grade 1 side, so you can give yourself a thumbs up for them. Or, maybe there are goals on that side that you want to work hard to include in your writing next time.

"How many of you think that this checklist has given you ideas for how you can make your story more powerful?" Many children so signaled.

LINK

Summarize today's minilesson, reminding writers that they already have their copies of "What Makes Writing Easy to Read," which works like a checklist as well. Then send children off to revise and write true stories.

"So, writers, today you have a new tool—you have a checklist that you can look at to make sure you are writing a really great story. *And* you also have our chart we have been using from the beginning of the unit, "What Makes Writing Easy to Read." This can also be used like a checklist, too, to help you make sure that your readers can read your amazing stories. You'll probably notice that some of items on the checklist we were just using are also here. This is because I *really* want people to be able to read your great stories."

"Today, I am going to watch you use both these checklists to first fix up your writing like Rufus had to fix up his—and remember, Rufus needed to write his all over again. I am pretty sure most of you will do that, too. And then you can start a whole new story. You can also use your copies of our 'What Makes Writing Easy to Read' list. Be reading it before you start so that you keep those things in mind as you write.

"Give me a thumbs up if you already know what you are going to do to make the story you are holding better." Those children were sent off to get started. "The rest of you, will you read your writing over and talk with each other about whether your writing does the things on this chart and about what you can do today?" I had soon channeled those writers to their writing spots as well.

I've found that many teachers resist the idea of writing a whole new draft, thinking that's asking a lot of a writer—especially of a kindergartner. Don't project your resistance onto your children. Keep in mind that writing a whole new draft is actually an easier alternative than moving to a whole new story! Meanwhile, redrafting is a critical form of revision.

Using the Narrative Writing Checklist to Inform Your Conferences and Small-Group Work

THE NARRATIVE WRITING CHECKLIST can be used as a helpful tool during your conferring to help you assess where your students currently stand in relation to the Common Core State Standards for narrative writing so that you can think about the areas in which they need the most support. For example, the checklist suggests that by the end of kindergarten, children should be able to look over their narrative writing (and you should be able to look over it as well) and say yes to the expectation that the story is written in order. As you look across the writers in your classroom, you may notice that there is a contingent of children still listing their thoughts about a topic rather than writing a narrative. Their so-called true stories might read, "I love Mom. Mom is my mom. My mom has brown hair." Such a text is not a narrative. If you have a

cluster of children who, when asked to write true stories, often produce texts with that list-like, all-about structure, then you may want to pull them together to learn the difference between an all-about book and a story, a narrative. You will certainly want to read stories to those children (and others) and to create opportunities for the children to story-tell episodes in their lives and to retell the stories they read.

Then, too, the checklist (and the CCSS) suggest that in kindergarten, children should learn to include not only the events that occurred, but the person's reaction. Again, it is helpful for you to carry this checklist with you—or an internalized version of it—and to triage your children so that you take note if there are some children who have yet to

---

MID-WORKSHOP TEACHING   Tapping Writers' Memories in Order to Add Details to Their Stories

"Writers, eyes up here. You will remember that on the checklist it says that story writers include *details* about what happens. Roberto was just writing a story about playing baseball, and after he wrote a bit he said, 'Oops. I gotta check on details about the people.' So he did something that really helped. He reread what he had written and remembered what happened. He reread"

> I threw the ball.
>
> My brother came and helped me.

"Then he looked up from the page like this and he said, 'I couldn't hold the ball right.'

"And you know what he did after that? He added that detail. 'I couldn't hold the ball right. My brother showed me.'

"So, writers, the checklist can tell you things to do, but sometimes, it's going to be other kids who give you ideas for how to actually do the thing. The checklist tells us to add details, but Roberto showed us one way to do this. One way to add details is to do like Roberto did, and reread the story, then remember it, and come up with tiny little true parts that aren't yet on the page.

"Do any of you think you could do that right now? Will you look at your story—the part that is on the

page right in front of you? Will you reread what you have written and then remember that time? And in your memory, look around. What do you see that you could add? You could add the details you see into the drawing or into the words. Do that right now."

To Lilly, I said, "Remember making that snowman? Look at your drawing, point to what is there on the page, and find things that you didn't yet draw. Then add them."

I got to Liam just as he was writing something with his pencil. I said to the class, "Liam searched for the missing stuff, and he found some and now he is writing more words into his story."

---

do this work. You'll again want to convene small groups with children who need help doing this. You may, for example, want to show children that there are expectations that some people have decided are important for kids their age. Start with a simple and accessible one. "You are expected to put your name on all your stories. Can you reread through your folder of stories and see if you have done that?" Then you can up the ante.

"You are expected to show how you felt about what happened." You might say, "Let's pretend we were writing a story about this conference, and we wanted to show how you feel about our conference. What might you draw to show that? What might you write?" Then you could help children look back at a finished book and determine whether they have already done this. You can help them to tackle the task by adding on an ending sentence or by adding facial expressions to a picture.

By first grade, children learn to write a beginning for their stories. You might carry some familiar books with you and show children the way other authors begin their books and suggest they create beginnings for all their completed stories. The power of a folder full of completed stories is that it gives youngsters repeated opportunities to work at something and develop proficiency at that work.

Obviously, if you find that it is not a small group of children needing help in any of these qualities of effective narrative writing but that instead, most of your children need such help, you'll want to do the instruction through either a minilesson, a mid-workshop, or a teaching share—or all three!

Reaching for New Narrative Writing Goals

Focus on a new item on the Narrative Writing Checklist.

"Writers, just like the pilot of that airplane, you have been working so hard today using a checklist to help you know what to do in your writing. Give yourselves a round of applause for all of this hard work!" I waited while the children cheered and clapped.

"Now I want to draw your attention to *one* item from our checklist. This one is about the way writers end their stories." I pointed to the checklist and read the fourth bullet on the grade 1 side: *After I wrote the last thing I did, I wrote how I felt about it.*

Rally students to use the new checklist item to assess a writing sample and then make plans for improvement.

"All right, let's take another look at my friend Rufus's writing. Pay careful attention to the ending." I read the writing to the class.

> It was snowy. I fed my rabbit. He is brown. He did not wake up. I touched him and he was dead.

"So what do you think? Did the story end with how Rufus felt about his rabbit dying? Let's see the thumbs up or thumbs down." I looked around the room to a sea of thumbs down. "You guys are right. Rufus's ending needs some work. He did not end his story with how he felt. Right now, turn to your partner and come up with some suggestions for Rufus, ways he could rewrite or add to his story now that he knows how stories should end." I gave the students a few moments to talk and then called the group back together. "Let's hear it! Suggestions for ways Rufus can rewrite his ending so that he ends with a feeling?"

"He was probably really sad," said Aiden. "Sad is a feeling, he could end it and say, 'I was sad.'"

"Maybe he was scared, like he didn't know what to do. He should say he was scared," volunteered Tyler.

"Nice suggestions, writers. You did such a great job using the checklist to help Rufus figure out that he needed to work on his ending. Tomorrow and every day when you go back to your writing, be sure to use this tool to help you make your writing the best that it can be!"

The Common Core State Standards actually word this a bit differently. There children are asked to include a reaction to what happened.

Session 7

A Vowel Chart Can Help with the Middles of Words

AS YOU WILL RECALL, the larger theme of this bend in the road of the unit is the idea that writers can rely on tools to help them accomplish their goals. You began the previous minilesson by showing children pictures of workers, using tools to help with heavy lifting and manual labor. You made the point that writers, too, use tools—not shovels and electric saws, but writerly tools.

Today you will teach children to use a vowel chart when they write. This, of course, is a subset of the alphabet chart that children learned to use earlier in the year, and you will want to continue to review the use of that chart, especially in small groups and conferences.

Specifically, in this session, you will put a spotlight on vowels. When it comes to listening to sounds in words and then writing the letters that make those sounds, vowels are the real tricksters. As we know, this is because vowels all make more than one sound. To make matters more challenging, vowels are also positional, and we have to help kindergartners understand that the sound the vowels make may depend on where they are in a word. And sometimes vowels are even silent. (Now, if that is not tricky, I do not know what is!)

Many of your kindergarten writers will not necessarily be ready for the work of listening for and putting a vowel in their words when they try to spell. Spelling development typically develops from the ability to hear and record a first sound in a word and then a last sound in a word and then on to the middle sounds in a word. At first, most of the sounds children hear are consonants. The Common Core Foundational Skills understand this progression and will ask us to build on students' phonemic awareness (CCSS RF.K.2). However, you can get your children to begin to hold the vowel space by giving them the information that every word has at least one vowel. Even if their vowel guess is incorrect, it does make the word they are writing look more like a conventional word.

Whether your word work uses a synthetic (the parts are taught directly and then put together to make wholes) or an analytic (the wholes are presented and then children take out the parts) approach to the teaching of phonics, you will most likely find it challenging to get kids to bring what they are learning in that part of their day to the spelling of words

IN THIS SESSION, you'll teach students that vowels help writers spell the middle of words. Using a vowel chart can help writers identify and come up with the right vowels to put on their paper.

GETTING READY

✔ Chart paper, marker (see Connection)

✔ Vowel chart, pointer (see Teaching and Active Engagement)

✔ An example of "Hard to Read" student writing that is missing vowels, enlarged on chart paper (see Teaching)

✔ Student writing folders, pencils (see Share)

✔ Magnetic letters for the vowels (see Connection)

COMMON CORE STATE STANDARDS: W.K.3, W.K.5, RFS.K.2d, SL.K.1, L.K.2.c, L.1.2.c

in the writing workshop. This session and sessions like the ones presented in this book are one answer to the problem of transfer. We encourage you to spotlight interactive writing, probably during entirely different times of the day. There are only six vowels, but they have major impact in the making of words. Ultimately, this focused work will help young writers feel more confident about making their stories readable for their audiences.

"Writing workshop is the reason to learn about words. In some ways, writing workshop is the game and word work time is the practice."

Even though this session involves showing your kids how to use their knowledge of how vowels work and their vowel chart to help them write more readable middles of words, this session is also about making word work highly engaging for kids. Writing workshop is *the* reason to learn about words. In some ways, writing workshop is the game and word work time is the practice. Without game day, practice is not very much fun or even very necessary.

In the end, you want the vowel work of this session to feel fun. The playful tone of your teaching needs to show your kids how cool it is to use these six letters to help make words better. You will know your teaching has gone well if your kids are asking, "Where might the vowels go in this word? Let's play around and see!"

Using the Power of Vowels to Write the Middles of Words

CONNECTION

Rally children to sing "Old MacDonald" with you, then point out that the chorus contains vowels. Introduce vowels to your children, altering the chorus of the song to reflect all vowels.

"Writers, how many of you know that song, 'Old MacDonald Had a Farm'?" Then I started to sing the song, with children joining in. I especially stressed the chorus—E-I-E-I-O.

One of the goals of the connection is to connect with youngsters—and with the topic of the day. This start to the minilesson does both!

"Writers, the really cool thing about that song is that it is not just a song about the animals that Old MacDonald has on his farm, like the cow and the sheep. It is also a song about letters. E-I-E-I-O.

"And this is the important thing. Those aren't just any ol' letters; they are called *vowels*. And vowels are the letters that all of us work the *hardest* to figure out. And I know you all love working hard to figure things out, right? When you are writing and want to spell a word, the vowels are usually the trickiest parts of words to spell. For that reason, I thought today we'd tackle the *hard work* part of spelling, if you are game. Are you?"

Note the life lesson that is being taught. Vowels are totally cool because we work hard to figure them out, and we love working hard!

The kids were absolutely with me, nodding their heads, showing their muscles, and generally rising to the occasion.

I continued on. "So the first thing you need to know is that the person who wrote that song didn't have her vowels quite straight. I know the song goes," and I wrote on chart paper, *E-I-E-I-O.* "But today I am going to give each of you a new tool—a vowel chart," which I distributed. "You will see that, in fact, the real true vowels are A-E-I-O-U. Let's sing that song again, and this time, sing the right vowels."

You'll want to recruit children to join in shared reading of chart often so they internalize it, just as they've internalized "Old MacDonald Has a Farm."

We did this, continuing through the song enough to reach the chorus several times.

A full-size version of the vowel chart is available on the CD.

❖ **Name the teaching point.**

"Today I want to teach you that vowels can help you spell the middles of words. If you know just a few tips about how vowels work, this can make your writing so much easier to read. A vowel chart can help you hear the vowel sound and come up with the right vowel to put on your paper."

TEACHING

Tell children about a child whose writing is hard to read, using a piece of kid writing that could be made more readable had the writer used vowels.

"My friend Roseanne has a daughter in kindergarten, like you guys. The other night, she brought me her daughter's writing, and she said, 'I can't read anything my daughter writes. She doesn't know *any* of her letters and sounds.' She showed me a story her daughter had written in school. One page went like this":

>   I dst with my sstr.

"I looked at the writing and I said to my friend, 'I can read it—and your daughter does too know *lots* of letters and sounds.'"

Then I said to the children, "Can you guys read it? Try—it's pretty hard."

Teach children that when words are hard to read and write, sometimes it is because of the tricky parts— vowels. It helps to know every word has a vowel and to guess which of them a word contains.

The children sounded the words out, mostly struggling. "I'm glad some of you are looking at the picture, because you are right that often the picture will give you some clues. But here is one more clue for you. Every word in the whole wide world has a vowel. So when it says 'I dst,' I know there has got to be a vowel that she left out (and remember, they are tricky, so kids often *do* leave them out). I knew it could contain any one of those five letters," and I sang, to the tune of "Old MacDonald," "A-E-I-O-U." Using the vowels, I recopied the writing, including many different options.

>   I dast with my sstr
>
>   I dest with my sster
>
>   I dist . . .

"Does that help any of you read her writing?" Some of the children grasped that yes, the story must require the first of those options—"I danced with my sister"—and we used the picture to confirm their guess.

When work is hard, it's good to have some tricks up our sleeves. This strategy isn't surefire—the writer could have inserted the missing vowel in a different part of the word to less effect—but the student is given a way to proceed that at least may well pay off.

This is the same work in reading. One strategy readers can use when they need to read a tricky word is to play around with different vowel sounds. They can try different sounds for a vowel and then confirm their guess by checking the picture and checking to see if it sounds like how we talk.

Recap by reminding students that when the middle of a word is hard, it is often because vowels are tricky. Using a vowel—any vowel—helps make writing more readable.

"Writers, I am telling you this because my knowledge of vowels helped me *read* that little girl's writing, and it can also help you *write* more readable writing. You need to remember that every word has at least one vowel (and those are the hardest parts of many words). So, when I read through my writing, I check to be sure I have written with vowels, with. . . ." and I sang, and the children joined in, "A-E-I-O-U. If a word doesn't have one of those letters, I know I don't have a finished word yet."

Show students how to use the vowel chart to help determine which vowel to use.

"I have one more tip. It is hard to decide which vowel, so when I am not sure, I use our vowel chart to help me figure out which vowel to use." I walked to where an enlarged chart hung. "We can read the chart to remind ourselves of the sounds that the different vowels make." With pointer in hand, I read, inviting children to join me, "A—apple—/a/, E—egg—/e/, I—igloo—/i/, O—octopus—/o/, U—umbrella—/u/.

"When I am trying to figure out which of these vowel sounds I hear in a word, I really stretch the part where the vowel might go and listen hard, and I also pay attention to how the sound feels in my mouth. Sometimes with vowels, it can be hard to *hear* the difference between one vowel and another, but you can *feel* the way the sound feels in your mouth, what the sound does to the mouth."

I said, "Daaaaaaanst," stretching it out, and as I did this I put one finger to my ear and another finger to my mouth. I said, "Remember to hear and *feel* the vowel sound as you say it. Then I take what I hear and feel to the vowel chart and I try to match it to one of the key word pictures. Once I find a sound match, then I know which vowel I might need.

"You think, 'Daaaaanst' sounds and feels most like /aaaaaaa/ as in *apple*? Yes or no?" I repeated the question so that more children could know that we needed an *a* in danced. Then I said, "Yes! We do need an *a* in *danced*. They match."

ACTIVE ENGAGEMENT

Invite the children to try using the vowel chart with partners. Together, they can help you add vowels to the problematic writing from earlier in the minilesson.

"So, writers, pretend this is your story, and you are rereading it. You have added the *a* into *danced*, so that word now has a vowel. Can you read on and see if your new tool can help you find a word that doesn't have a vowel?"

Soon the children were calling out that *sstr* didn't have a vowel. They knew the letters were an attempt at writing *sister*. "Let's figure out what the vowel could be," I said. "Remember, warm up by rereading the vowel chart, then say the word and stretch out the part where the vowel goes. Stretch that part out, hear and feel the sound, and finally, match the sound to the vowel on the chart that makes that sound. Turn to your partner. Go."

Teachers, when you are teaching writing, don't forget about word families! There are thirty-seven words families that can help kids spell about 500 words. The word families help kids make C-V-C words and also teach children a foundational spelling strategy. These words help teach your writers that one known word can help you spell other unknown words. Spelling by analogy depends on a child's ability to see patterns and to hear rhymes. If a child cannot hear that "fit" and "sit" sound the same, then it will be very difficult for them to use the -IT family to help them spell the word "split." It is definitely more efficient to write words using word chunks, and word family knowledge helps children do that work. Also, once your writers understand a word family, sometimes they can then begin to recognize that short vowel sound in other words, too.

I leaned in to listen to two partnerships at the same time. Emily and Sophia were just talking about how they already knew how to spell the word *sister*. I said, "You guys are right. You don't need to do this stretching and matching work with vowels if a word is a snap word for you. But, I want you to practice these steps because I think you will probably come to a word soon and not be able to figure out the vowel." I left as Emily and Sophia were trying the steps for writing with vowels.

Victor and Tyler were really stretching their vowels. I just leaned in and tapped my mouth and my ear with my fingers. "Hear and feel," I said to them.

Convene the class and summarize what you saw children doing in order to use their new tool, the vowel chart.

"Guys, look up. I saw so many of you working to put the power of vowels in your words. This is what I saw. I saw kids warming up using their vowel charts. I saw kids super-stretching *sister*, like this—siiiiiiiister—trying to hear and feel the sound, and I saw you trying to match that sound with one of the vowels from your charts."

"So many of you thought the missing vowel was an *i*," and I wrote it into the word on the page.

LINK

Send children off with a reminder to use all that they know about making their writing easier to read, every time they write.

"Writers, I think you are ready to get started writing another true story today! Wow, your backpack of strategies to make your writing easier to read just keeps getting more and more full! Pretty soon it will be overflowing. Don't forget that now in *addition* to all that you already were doing to write powerful stories and to make readable writing, you can now use your vowel chart to help you with the tricky letters."

While it is not necessary to add to the anchor chart in front of the class or even refer to it in every lesson, be sure to add this strategy, "Be sure every word has a vowel," to the chart at some point.

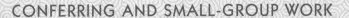

Coaching Students to Do the Hard Work, and Not Doing It for Them

ALTHOUGH YOU HAVE JUST GIVEN WRITERS A NEW TOOL and are apt to find yourself swept up in the effort to implement that tool, remember that your conferences do not have to match the minilesson but should, instead, provide support for youngsters to draw upon all they have learned across the entire unit.

And in the spirit of first things first, you will probably want to start your work by making sure that children are finding it easy to progress from finishing one story to starting another. Are they putting their finished work behind a red-dotted portion of their writing folder? Are they returning to pieces that are not quite done, always finishing them up before moving on? Are they producing something close to a story a day?

The important thing is that writers can proceed along, working with productivity and not requiring your participation to end one piece and start the next. Expect that after finishing one story, children will immediately get themselves a blank booklet and begin the process of touching the pages and saying their next story aloud, then sketching the story, then writing it. Some may still be writing lots of labels, probably in addition to some approximation of a story, written in sentences. Many will have moved toward writing sentences.

You should not find that many of your children suffer from writer's block. Most young children simply run their minds over the things they've been doing lately, and something surfaces as a potential story. The child fell off the monkey bars, or walked home from school, or ate an ice cream cone, or walked her dog, or a million other small events. Coach children to think, "What did I do first?" and then to sketch that. "Then what happened?" Ask, "How did it end?" Because writing is slow for children, you provide enormous support simply by rereading what the child has written so far, doing so in a storytelling voice, accumulating the pages so that the writer hears the sequence of the story.

MID-WORKSHOP TEACHING
Including Vowels in Every Part of a Word

"Writers, today we talked about how every word has a vowel in it. That tip is going to get even more complicated, if you are ready to learn more." The children suggest they are game. "Long words like *di-no-saur* and *cat-er-pil-lar* have parts, or syllables, in them. *Di-no-saur* has three parts, or three syllables. /Di/, that's one, /no/, that's the second syllable, and /saur/, that's the third one! Well, here is *another* tip. Each part (or syllable) of a word has a vowel in it. Let's work together to figure out the vowels for each part of the word *dinosaur*, okay?"

I called out the first syllable. "'Di.' What do you hear? Turn and tell your partner what vowel sound you hear in the first syllable. Don't forget, you can use the vowel chart to help you!" I listened in as the children chatted with their partners, then called the group back together. "I heard you all stretching out the first part of *dinosaur*, and guess what? After listening to all of you, I think I know what vowel belongs in the first syllable. An *i*!" We continued through the other two syllables.

"Today, Liam noticed a word in his own writing that had more than one part to it. When he was writing the word *baseball*, he realized that he had written one vowel, an *a*. But, he also could hear two claps in his word, and so he knew that it had two parts. Two parts means at least two vowels. Liam wrote the word *baseball* like this, 'basbal.' Bravo, Liam!"

(continues)

Remember, if you already know a word, just write it, but make sure it has a vowel. And, if you (like Victor and Tyler) are having trouble deciding which vowel to put in the word, you can just pick one and put it there to hold the vowel place. Having a vowel in a word, even an incorrect one, is better than not having a vowel at all." And "if you hear a vowel letter's name when you super-stretch a word, then write that letter. For instance, Aiden was trying to write the word *paper*, and when he super-stretched the word, he heard the name of the letter *a*—paaaaaper. He wrote an *a* after the first letter, *p*." (If you want to teach the long vowel concept through a song like you did in the minilesson, you might sing 'Apples and Bananas': "I like to eat, eat, eat, apples and bananas. I like to ate, ate, ate, apples and bananas . . .".

When helping a child reread his or her writing, remember that you don't want to do most of the work for the child. Move alongside the writer as he or she works. Interject lean, concise prompts that remind the writer what to do. Imagine how a coach interacts with his athletes in the heat of competition. Hours have been spent practicing and preparing. The coach and the athlete have already talked in some detail about work the athlete needs to do. But now, in the heat of competition, the coach resorts to lean prompts that remind the athlete of all he or she knows. All that's needed to remind the boxer not to pop her head up is the call "Chin down . . . chin down . . ." and you'll give similar prompts to writers.

That is, in a coaching conference, you will not want to talk on and on about what you hope the writer will do. Instead, you watch the writer at work and insert succinct prompts. The writer wants to write *dinner* and has written a *d*. Now the writer sits, paralyzed, unsure of what comes next. Just say, "Reread with your finger," or "Point under the words," and later, "Did it match?"

If the child has trouble, you can decide to demonstrate. "Watch how I reread with my finger," you might say, but again, you will soon want to pass the baton back to the child. "Now you do it," you'll say.

It is key to allow approximation. If you realize that the child who is writing "dinner" doesn't know the *er* chunk, you need to decide whether this is within reach for that child right now. Chances are good it is not. But even if you believe the child should know this chunk, you need not make a fuss about this right here and now. For now, you might decide to help this child make progress in his work, and so you might just tuck away your intention to teach the *er* chunk, saving it at for another time.

Remember, it is important to leave your writer with a strategy that will become part of his or her repertoire that will carry over into the rest of his writing life.

FIG. 7–1 Alexa's story. I went apple picking. My father was in front of us. My father got to the top of the hill before us. My father kicked apples down the hill. Me and my brother laughed. We kept on walking and my father kept on kicking apples. My father kept on kicking apples down the hill. Me and my brother kept on laughing. My father kept on kicking.

Checking for Vowels

Channel writers to review writing in the finished portion of their folders, making sure those old pieces of writing contain vowels in every word.

"Guys, bring your folders with you." Once children had gathered, I said, "This is a good time to use what you learned about vowels today, to help make the writing you have done on other days more readable. You have a bit of time now to study one of your finished stories. Be on the lookout for whether you have a vowel in every word and even every syllable. If it doesn't, try to get a vowel into that word. Ready . . . go!"

Each child began to reread an old story and hunt for vowels. Just as kindergarten children so often do, they called out as they discovered things about their own writing.

"I don't have no vowels," Riley said.

"You don't have *any* vowels," I repeated and smiled. I directed her toward the vowel chart.

The room was filled with vowel writers, and as I looked at the words where the vowels were landing, I could easily see that this new vowel power made a big difference for my writers.

I said, "Writers, I am going to stop you now, but I want you to know that this is work you can continue first thing tomorrow. Remember, the work of this unit is to make writing that other people can really read. So, as we learn new things, you'll want to go back some to old writing. Hey, that's it! As we keep learning more let's use the new stuff to make our whole folders full of pieces easier and easier and easier to read."

Writing Readable Stories Using Word Walls

SO FAR IN THIS PORTION OF THE UNIT, you have equipped your writers with several tools that will help them make their writing easier to read. Today, you supply one more, an especially important tool: the word wall. This will be an alphabetically organized section of your classroom wall on which you display perhaps twenty (for now) high-frequency words that are especially accessible for kindergarten children and that will give them a lot of writing and reading power. Your message to children will be that when they want to write one of those words—say, the word *the*—instead of stretching out the word and recording the sounds, it helps to think, "Oh! I just know that word," and then to write it in a snap.

Of course, for kindergartners, you are not just teaching them the repertoire of high-frequency words—and the value of knowing a bunch of such words can't be overestimated—you are also teaching these children that not *all* words need to be spelled in a letter-by-letter fashion. Sometimes, writers start to write a word and think, "I know that!" and then presto, the word is on the page. Obviously, the more words a writer can write without having to slow down and stretch them out, the more fluency she will have as a writer (this is true for her reading as well!).

It is important for children to develop a repertoire of words they can spell and read without applying any word-solving strategies. Researcher Sandra Wilde found that half the words our children read and write are the same thirty-six words. Most children will learn these words from many encounters with them, but we can hasten this process by teaching some of these words directly. You'll probably devote twenty minutes each day to word study (as well as more to interactive writing and so forth, where children apply what they learn in word study), and you'll probably use a portion of this time to teach children new high-frequency words. If you teach a few new high-frequency words each week during word study time, you can then devote some minilessons to teaching children that writers use the high-frequency words they already know to help them tackle unfamiliar words. Teach children that if they know *like*, they can easily write *bike*. Many high-frequency, or "word wall words," give writers the word-power to read and write other words.

IN THIS SESSION, you'll teach students that writers rely heavily on words they know in a snap in order to make their writing more readable.

GETTING READY

✓ Personal word walls for each student, which includes words from the class word wall (see Teaching) ✏️

✓ Easel

✓ Student writing folders (see Active Engagement)

✓ Small Post-it notes for students (see Active Engagement)

✓ Chart paper, marker (see Share)

✓ "How to Turn a Word into a Snap Word" chart (see Share)

COMMON CORE STATE STANDARDS: W.K.3, W.K.5, RFS.K.3.c, SL.K.1, L.K.1.b,c; L.K.2.c,d; L.1.2.d

You will want to preface all of this instruction with "I noticed many of you are having some trouble writing the word _____" so that your children know spelling matters for one big reason: we need to spell words so people can read our writing.

"Children need to know spelling matters for one big reason: we need to spell words so people can read our writing."

In this session, you'll remind children that they can write some words in a snap, without sounding them out. You'll also give each child their own personal word wall. These personal word walls can hold an ever growing repertoire of classroom-taught high-frequency words, making this a mini-version of your word wall. The personal word wall can also hold any other words that individual children can spell in a snap, such as names of family and friends or words that children have learned from their reading of books and of the world. There will be different words on the word wall in first grade or second grade as children outgrow themselves as spellers.

Writing Readable Stories Using Word Walls

CONNECTION

Tell writers that you are proud of all of the hard work they are doing to make their writing so readable and powerful.

"The work you did yesterday figuring out how to get more vowels in your words was truly amazing. As I watched all of you do that work, I started to think you had the hearts of fighters. Fighters don't give up, even when it feels like the fight is too hard. There were moments yesterday when it looked like the fight for vowels might be too hard, but you kept trying. I so admired your hearts as I watched.

"As I made my way home from school last night, I was thinking about how you guys, in kindergarten, already know that writing is hard work. It is—and then I started to worry. I started to worry that if something was all hard work all of the time, would you all be able to keep at it with a fighter's heart always? I asked myself, 'If writing is a fight every minute, won't my writers start to run out of energy before they have a chance to tell their true stories?'"

Tell writers that writing is not always hard work. There are many words that writers just know.

"Then it hit me. Writing words so that other people can read them *can* be hard work at times, but it is not *always* hard work. It is not always hard work because there are many words writers just know and therefore don't have to fight for.

"I started to think that it would fill you with energy if I help you become more aware of all of the words you already know, all of the words you can write in a snap and don't have to fight so hard for."

❖ **Name the teaching point.**

"Today I want to teach you that every writer has words that he or she just knows and can write easily, in a snap. Writers don't stretch out those words—they just write them quickly. Word walls are a great tool for writers because they remind writers of the words they know in a snap."

Again, this minilesson begins with revisiting the intense hard work the children did the preceding day. The children also hear their teacher's been thinking about them. "As I made my way home from school last night, I was thinking about how you guys. . . ." That's a powerful message: I take you home with me. I think about you all day long.

TEACHING

Show your writers how a word wall works.

I held up my personal word wall—a duplicate of the class word wall, only instead of squishing everything onto one side of the paper, the word wall was distributed across two sides of a page. (See CD for an example of a personal word wall.)

"So, writers, I have my own personal word wall here, and I have one of these for each of you as well." I distributed personal word walls to each child. "Our word walls already have the exact same words that we have on our classroom word wall. The words are organized under their starting letter. So, if I want to find the word *me*, I'd look under *m*. See if you can find *me* on your word walls with your finger." They did.

"Good. Each word is written under the letter it begins with."

Demonstrate how you make a personal word wall even more personal by modeling with one student in the class.

"Right now, we each have the same word wall. But we can make each person's word wall more personal by adding some of the words that each of us knows how to spell in a snap. There will be different words that I know in a snap and that you each know.

"So, let's work together to help Simon make his word wall into a more personal one. Simon, why don't you come up here with your word wall and sit next to me?" Simon leaped to the front of the room and sat down in the chair I had pulled next to mine. "Simon, let's take your word wall and clip it right to the easel so that we can add your own personal words to it, okay?" I attached Simon's word wall to the easel.

"Okay, Simon, if we are going to make a personal word wall for you, we need to think about the words you use a lot, the ones you can spell in a snap. These are the words that you don't need to stretch out because you just know how to spell them in a snap," and I snapped my fingers for emphasis. "It helps to think, 'What are some things I write about a lot?' That question can help a writer remember words that the writer just knows. What would you say you write about a lot, Simon?"

Simon pondered my question for a minute, then brightened. "I know," he said. "I write about my family. So I know words like *mom* and *dad* and I know how to spell my sister's name, *Annie*. And I like to write about my *Nana* and *Poppa*, too, so I know how to spell them." He was quiet a moment, then added, "And bikes. We ride bikes in the park a lot, so I can spell *bike*." A child in the meeting area suggested, "And *park*?" and Simon confirmed that word as well.

"Fantastic, Simon! I am going to add those words to your personal word wall to remind you that these are words that you just know in a snap. You can just write the letters down fast on the page. You don't have to spend the time stretching them out, because you just know them!" I added these words to Simon's personal word wall, under the appropriate letters.

Many teachers dress up children's personal word walls by sliding each one into a plastic sleeve. That way, as children learn more and the word walls change, new word walls can be slid on top of old ones.

It has always seem to us that m *is the easiest letter to teach. Its sounds and its name of the same. One can say* m *for a long time and still be saying* m *(try that with* k*, for example, and you'll see you are soon saying a vowel). Most of all,* m *is important when writing* me *or* Mom. *And McDonald's is represented by a golden* M.

ACTIVE ENGAGEMENT

Give students an opportunity to read through their writing, searching for their own personal words they know in a snap.

"Would each of you take a story out of your writing folder and be on the lookout for words that you just know. Just like Simon, those snap words are probably things or places or people you know well and write about a lot. When you find a word you can just write in a snap, stick one of the Post-its right near that word. Then later on, when you go back to get started on your writing, you can write those words on your personal word wall. Use the first letter of that word to help you know where to put it."

I moved among the writers, helping them notice just how many words they could already write without needing to sound them out.

"Guys, would you put your folders and word walls on the floor in front of you? I want to do a little more teaching before I send you off to your writing work today." I waited for some stillness. "Post-its down, too, please."

LINK

Caution writers that the word wall is not a source of story ideas, with writers simply linking high-frequency words together. Writers first generate story ideas, referring to the word wall only for spelling.

Holding up the personal word wall we created for Simon, I said, "So, soon, each of you will have a personal word wall like Simon has. The word wall is yours because it has your special snap words. What I want you to remember now is that whenever you are reading or writing, you can collect more words for your word wall. Your word wall will keep growing as you do this.

"Before you go off to write with this new tool, I want to make sure I teach you how to use this tool to help you get your ideas down on the paper. What you *don't* want to do is use the words on your word wall to help you decide what story you want to tell. You always start with the true story that happened to you." I pointed to my bumblebee story as I said, "This really happened to us one day in class, and so when we started to write about this, we started by remembering what happened. Then we drew the pictures and decided on the words to tell that story. Just before we write, it can help to think, 'Wait, are some of the words on my word wall?' and that way, we write those words in a snap."

Send children off with a reminder to personalize their word walls and then use them as a resource while they write.

"So, writers, today you will first make your word wall by looking back at your stories and bringing the words you use a lot and know how to spell to your word wall. Then think of a great story to write. Off you go!"

You might want to have kids put Post-its on words they think they spell in a snap and then you can confirm that they are indeed correctly spelled before kids copy them onto their word walls.

When you teach children new high-frequency words, you are teaching them a process for imprinting new words onto their brain. For this reason, it is wise to progress through the same sequence of steps with each new high-frequency word. Once children have taken a mental picture of lots of high-frequency words, they should be able to do this on their own.

It is wise to have children reread what they've written and begin adding onto it before they refer to the word wall. This will make it unlikely that the word wall determines the content of their writing. You don't want a list of words to influence the content of your children's writing! Sometimes a few children see the word wall as a way to write without having to sound out so many words—which in a way it is—but these writers can get into some trouble if they end up basing their ideas for stories on the words that happen to be on the word wall!

Increasing Students' Sight Word Knowledge

EVEN THOUGH THIS IS A BOOK ABOUT TEACHING WRITING, because reading and writing are reciprocal processes, the work you do in writing often pays off in reading gains, too. For this reason, sometimes, conferences and small-group work with kindergarten students involve practicing word work. Because sight words are absolutely critical to learning to read (and write), you will probably want to pull some small groups or do some one-on-one teaching to increase the store of sight words your kindergarten students have at their disposal.

Most of our pedagogy around sight words comes from Linnea Ehri's work in *Scientific Studies of Reading*. Before you can imagine the small-group work that can increase sight word knowledge, you must first understand what sight words are, why they are important, and the typical phases of sight word development. To understand how to effectively apply her work, it is necessary to have some background on Ehri's ideas.

According to Ehri, sight words are not limited to high-frequency or irregularly spelled words. Rather, Ehri articulates, "Any word that is read sufficiently often becomes a sight word that is read from memory" (2005, 169). Because sight words are read as wholes and from memory, the reader need not divert attention and effort from meaning making to word reading. Increased sight word knowledge makes reading more efficient and increases attention to the work of understanding a text. It makes sense then that working to increase a child's sight word knowledge could pay off in increased writing fluency and more meaning-filled writing. In a way, sight words could be seen as one of the most important factors in improving both the readability and the significance of a piece of writing. If kindergartners' brains are freed up to pay closer attention to fewer words in order to write them, there can be more brain space left to attend to the strategies students have learned to make higher-quality writing.

So how do children learn to read sight words? Sight word reading is a connection-forming process. Readers learn to read sight words by forming connections between letters in spellings and sounds in pronunciation of words. The connections happen out of the reader's knowledge of the alphabetic system.

MID-WORKSHOP TEACHING Persistent Rereading Can Produce Words that Bubble and Burst on the Page

"As I look around the room, I am noticing tons of writers using their word walls! You are not wasting any time stretching out words that you know in a snap. And, oh my goodness, I want to tell you all about something else I saw. I just watched Lilly say 'bubbling' five times! She was writing about swimming and wanted to tell about how she breathes, so she wanted to write, *Bubbling*. Lily tried to spell the start of it: /b/ /b/. She wrote that. Then she said, 'Buuuuuuuuubling,' and wrote the next sound. She ended up saying the word *five times* before she got all the sounds down. If any of the rest of you have written a great big wonderful and true word like that, a word that really helps your writing come alive, will you find it and make a fireworks celebration beside the word? Just use your pen to create some stars and explosions to celebrate because it is so cool when you do that. Nice going, Lilly, and nice going anyone else who has written one of those great, long, gorgeous words! Snap words *and* gorgeous words! I am impressed!"

Pre-alphabetic-phase readers don't use letter-sound knowledge to help them read words. If they read words at all, they do so by remembering selected visual features of words. A child is still a pre-alphabetic reader if he can read his name by the shape of the letters and knows the names of the letters when he chants them like a song, in order. Children at this stage are also just starting to connect sounds to those letters. Many of your kindergarten students will begin the year in this phase of word reading.

So, your first kind of group work during writing workshop might involve teaching the connection between letters and sounds. For instance, based on your assessment of your kids' letter-sound knowledge, you might do some work with magnetic letters making words. The more your students increase their understanding of the alphabetic system by understanding how letters and sounds work in words, the better able they will be to accumulate words they can read by memory.

Next comes the partial alphabetic phase. By the time you teach this unit, this will be a common stage in your classroom. Your children will use letters and sounds to read words, but they will use only parts of words at first—like beginnings and endings. They can form partial representations of words because they have not yet learned to segment all of the phonemes in a word, and they don't know about vowels (unless you stimulate the growth of vowels by introducing and playing with them).

At this stage, it seems like your kindergarten students can benefit from conferences where you notice and name the words they are spelling correctly. What you are doing is you are telling the child, "Hey, this is a sight word for you! If you see this combination of letters anywhere, read this word. And, if you want to write this word again, use these exact letters." Remember, increasing the number of words that are sight words pays off big for beginning writers.

This work is even more valuable if you can turn that known word into an anchor to aid with decoding and analogizing (two of the other three ways to read unknown words). For example, to help with decoding, if a child writes s-t-o-p for the word stop in his or her story, you first need to tell the student that it is correct. Then you can take it further. "That beginning s-t starts other words. St- st- still or st-st- stay or st-st- . . ." Then let

the child try to fill in a word of his or her own. Make sure you do a quick try to write and then read a word each using that s-t. You may ask, "What is this word?" Have the child read s-t-i-l-l. Then ask the child to try writing the word stay. To use this same personal sight word to assist analogy-based reading, teach the child that stop can help them write a bunch of other words. Have the child generate some words that rhyme. Then have him or her try to spell and read using the known to help with the unknown.

Children become full-phase alphabetic spellers when they can learn sight words by forming complete connections between letters in spellings and phonemes in pronunciations. So, the more writers know about the alphabetic system, the better able they are to learn and retain sight words. And finally, there is the consolidated phase. Once kids know more and more sight words, their knowledge gets consolidated into larger chunks. While these final two phases do not typically happen for most kindergarten students this early in the school year, knowledge of how this development occurs will help you focus and angle your teaching toward more sophisticated work.

All of this understanding about sight words should convince you of the importance of word work during writing workshop. However, we do want you to remember that word work is not the only kind of work writers need during small groups and during conferences. Balance is always the answer in our teaching if we are going to grow balanced writers and readers. What spelling stage do you think Colleen is in (see Figure 8–1)? She is probably ready to write more. She has a lot of sight words to increase fluency and ease of writing. (She also needs to stop spending her word writing energy on labels and instead spend that energy on sentence writing.)

One day I go out in the snow with my mommy.

Then I get hot cocoa mix.

Finally, we go home! And drink the hot cocoa!

FIG. 8–1 Notice the number of labels in her drawing.

Building Knowledge of High-Frequency Words

Guide students step by step through the process of learning new high-frequency words, starting by asking children to make observations about the new word.

After the writers convened, I said, "Writers, you did a lot of writing. How many of you finished a whole story today?" After most writers signaled yes, I continued, "You were able to write a lot partly because when you know words in a snap, your writing can be quick. That allows you to think something and then write it, lickety-split, writing just as quickly as you think.

"Here is the news that I want to tell you. The more words you know in a snap, the more you can write. The words you know by heart (or almost know by heart so they are on your word wall) give you word power. So it is really important for you to add more words to your personal word wall every day. Right now, I am going to teach you the learning steps you can follow anytime you want to add a new word to the word wall.

"I think the word *will* is a word that can come in handy for you. We use *will* when we talk about what we *will* do next, after this, in the future. We *will* go to lunch later. We *will* have recess. And soon, we *will* learn to spell *will*. Let me write it for you." I did. "As you know, whenever we try to learn a new word, we first study it, so let's do that now.

"Look at *will* and tell someone near you what you notice." The children talked, then I accumulated their observations by asking, "What are you noticing?"

"It starts with a *w*. Not that many words do."

"It's got two short letters and two tall guys."

"There are *two l*s at the end of the word. Weird."

Now ask students to fix the word into their visual memory.

"Good noticings. So when you want to learn a word for your word wall, you first need to look carefully at the word."

Now ask students to fix the word into their visual memory.

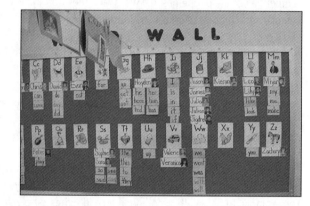

FIG. 8–2

"Now let's do the second step. Let's make a picture of the word in our minds. Let's look at the word as if our minds were cameras, and let's try to take a mental picture of it." Pretending to hold a camera, I pointed to the word, and said, "Click. Take a picture in your mind so you remember it for always."

Now, covering the word, I said, "Can you *still* see it in your mind, because that's the goal? When you close your eyes, what do you see?"

"I see dark and black when I close my eyes," Shavon said.

I laughed and said, "When you close your eyes and think of the word *will*, can you picture the letters? Try writing them on your hand. That is the third step, writing the word.

"Now, finally, check what you have pretend-written by looking up at the spelling and comparing to see if your letters match the letters on the board for the word." The children did this.

"When you go home and you are almost asleep and think, *will*, try to remember how to write that word in a snap. Next week, I am hoping this word will be stuck in your head like glue. Once you do the work, you need to make sure that you know the word forever. Let's all add *will* to our personal word walls."

How to turn a word into a Snap word

1. Look at it carefully.
2. Take a picture of it.
3. Write it.
4. Check it.

Writing Stories with True Words

Making Stories Talk

IN THIS SESSION, you'll teach students that writers include storytelling words in their writing.

GETTING READY

✔ Two examples of a story, one effectively using the word wall and one that ineffectively splices words together (see Connection)

✔ Draft of shared writing (see Teaching and Active Engagement)

✔ Example of student writing where storytelling language was used (see Share)

E XPERIENCED TEACHERS KNOW that teaching is a balancing act. You teach youngsters to write with exclamation marks, and soon you are reminding them that it is not necessary to use ten gigantic exclamations or to write exclamations after every third sentence. So it should not be surprising that when you teach youngsters that they can spell a set of known words easily, in a snap, and equip them with pages that list those words, some children will respond by overdoing their reliance on those high-frequency words. They'll string one word wall word together with the next, prioritizing correctness over everything else. You needn't be overly dismayed at this, but you do want to firmly channel youngsters back toward writing vibrant true stories.

This session, then, reminds you of your own power as a teacher. It reminds you that the instruction you have already given children in the importance of having a bank of words that one knows by heart can backfire, disabling rather than enabling your students. (The same thing happens in reading when kids begin to believe that accuracy is the only thing that matters. They become word callers, letting go of all attentiveness to story.)

Our aim in this session is to counter the prior emphasis on spelling by spotlighting the importance of vibrant stories, told with language that has the lilt and authenticity of oral language. In today's session, children will use their partners to help them write true stories.

The session also highlights the importance of listening, because everyone has had the experience of starting to talk to someone and finding that person's eyes roaming the room as you talk. Your energy for the story dissipates. You cut the corners, leave out the details, and reach the ending line quickly. On the other hand, everyone has also had the experience of telling a story to a rapt listener, and finding, as you talk, that details well up in you, that the whole event seems especially rich as you put it into words. As poet, Michael Rosen once said, "Stories happen to those who tell them."

This session, then, is about writing with courage, with a commitment to communicating with more rich, real language and doing this in ways that align to the Common Core State Standards with its emphasis on language (L.K.1, L.K.4).

COMMON CORE STATE STANDARDS: W.K.3, W.1.3, RFS.K.3.c, SL.K.1, SL.K.4, SL.K.6, SL.1.4, L.K.1, L.K.4, L.K.6

Writing Stories with True Words
Making Stories Talk

CONNECTION

Contrast a vacuous story, made by splicing word wall words together, with a vibrant story, in which the word wall is referred to only on an as needed basis.

"Writers, which of these would be a better story? Here's one." I told my story and the students listened:

> This weekend a boy named Kyrol visited me. He just recently moved to this country. He decided to make cookies—but he didn't know how! To make the cookies, he dotted lumps of cookie dough on a WOODEN cutting board, not on a metal cookie pan. In the oven, the wooden cutting board caught on fire, and soon flames were pouring out of the oven.

"Here is the other story," and I eyed the word wall board, obviously relying on it for each word that I used, as I told my story to the class:

> A boy made food in a pan. The pan got on fire. The oven had fire.

The children chimed in that the second story was boring. "You know something? In both stories, the boy cooks and sets the house on fire. So why is one story so much more interesting than the other?"

Recruit kids to inquire into how the one story was made differently than the other, growing their own conclusions about what does and does not work when writing stories.

"So here is the mystery that I want you all to try to solve. I'm going to give you only one minute to talk with anyone you want and solve the mystery. You ready? Here is the mystery. How did I go about writing the boring story that *didn't* work? And how did I go about writing the interesting story that *did* work? And what lessons can you learn for your writing? Listen again to the two stories"—I read quickly again—"and then talk about it!"

The room was filled with a hubbub of talk. I went to a few partnerships that needed a boost and acted out how I wrote the boring story so they could articulate what I did—finding and linking words from the word wall.

This is a true story about a boy, adopted at age eight, who problem solves as best he can, but ends up sometimes in hair-raising adventures. The best thing about telling true stories from one's own life is that the youngsters see your investment in these stories and this kindles commitment.

Orchestrate a grand conversation among children about the inquiry they've just engaged in.

"What did you discover?" I asked. I allowed the class to have a grand conversation about it, even though we don't usually do that in a minilesson. For a few minutes, one child after another pitched in:

"Your boring story was a word wall story!" Kevin said. "It wasn't the real story you would tell me usually."

"Yeah, and you said 'food' not 'cookies,' but it was cookies. We need cookies in the story," Lilly called.

"Your good story was good!" Zoe proclaimed.

"Because. . . ." I prompted with a grin.

"Because it was about telling the story true with the real words that really happened, like *cutting board* and *kitchen*. You didn't worry about using words that were definitely gonna be stretch words. You just told a good story."

"Writers, you almost named today's teaching point!"

❖ **Name the teaching point.**

"Today, we are learning that writers need to write with their own true, storytelling words even though that means they have to work a little harder to spell those true words. It helps to story-tell your story to your partner, using your best storytelling voice. Listen to your own storyteller voice, and put that voice onto the page."

TEACHING

Recruit children to join you in writing the last page to your ongoing story. Pretend you are doing this, only demonstrate the problematic way to write, relying exclusively on word wall words. Then recruit children to protest that that's the wrong way to proceed.

"Let's work together to use true storytelling words to write the ending to our bumblebee story. We already wrote most of the story. So let's reread it":

Page 1: During math, we sat on the rug. A bumblebee flew in the window.

Page 2: The bee flew toward us. We were scared.

Page 3: The bee went above our heads and landed right on the chart paper.

"Okay, so that is our story so far, and now we need to write what happened next. Hmmm. Watch me and tell me if you think I am doing a great job getting a true and lively story." I picked up a pen and said, "Hmmm. I want to make this so kids can read it." I looked up at the word wall, in an exaggerated fashion, touching a word or two, and then wrote:

> The bee

("I can spell that," I muttered under my breath . . .)

I paused. "It dove toward Simon, but I can't write *dove*. It . . . it . . ." Again I scrutinized the word wall. Then I added to the story:

> The bee is not nice. The bee goes up.

Recruit children to articulate what was wrong with the way you'd gone about writing, then re-articulate the goal that writers use their own storytelling voice to write.

I paused for the children's response, and they called out that the story was boring, that I had to use true storytelling words.

ACTIVE ENGAGEMENT

Recruit the children to provide a more positive example of writing that incorporates true storytelling words. Channel them to work with a partner to story-tell the shared episode that has been the source of the class story.

"Writers, how about if you all take a turn at this and try to do better than I did," I said. "Let's first remember that ferocious bee. Who remembers what that bee did?" Many hands went up. "Let's get the story straight in our minds because that's what writers do, right? Imani, will you be the bee, over by the window, and show us what you did, and the rest of you, watch and think about the true words you want to say to capture what that mean bee did. You ready, Imani? Observers ready? You are going to watch and try to put the true storytelling words to what the bee did."

Imani had meanwhile taken her place by the window, arms stretched straight behind her like wings. She leaped into the space at the front of the meeting area, spun around, and then dive-bombed straight at Simon, who swatted at her.

Recruit the class to co-construct the last page of the story, using storyteller language.

Notice that the same story is threading its way throughout many of our minilessons. It works well to return to the same familiar story because it's possible to zoom in on the issue at hand, to just focus on whatever the minilesson spotlights.

Notice that to make a positive point, we make a negative point. We show what not to do as a way to highlight what we hope writers will do.

It's amazing how a bit of drama can recruit children's energy. "Imani, will you be the bee, over by the window, and show us what you did. . . ." Suddenly, presto! Everyone's engaged.

"Okay, stop the action," I called, before the bee did any real damage rolling on the floor with Simon, the victim. "Partner 1, turn and tell Partner 2 the exact story of what happened. I'll read what we already wrote and you continue, writing in the air the words you would write."

> A bumblebee flew in our window. We looked up from the rug. The bee flew toward us. We were scared. The bee flew above our heads.

I leaned in to listen to Justin, who said, "The bee *went* to the front of the meeting area." I interrupted. "Can you find a more exact word for how the bee traveled?"

"Zigzagged?" Justin asked. Soon others had added more specific words to describe the bee's treatment of Simon. I reconvened the whole class by saying, to everyone and no one in particular, "How should this page go? Make sure you use your real true storytelling voice." To get them going, I again reread the story and soon they'd written this:

> A bumblebee flew in our window. We looked up from the rug. The bee flew toward us. We were scared. The bee flew above our heads. It zigzagged to the meeting area where it spun around until it saw Simon. It dove right at him. Simon swatted the bee away.

LINK

Remind students to incorporate storytelling language into their writing and to use their writing partner as a resource.

"So, writers, you have learned lots of ways to get hold of the true storytelling words of your stories. When you draw pictures, you can say the words that you want to write later, and doing that helps you remember those words. And then before you write, when you remember what happened and almost act it out, like Imani did for us, the writer thinks, 'What are the true words I can use to write that?' Now, here is the final challenge. Once you are writing the words, if you come to a word like *zigzagged*, what do you do?"

The children chimed that the writer stretches it out, listens for sounds. "And what if you come to a word like *will* . . . the bee *will* come back?" The children again talked, remembering that this was a word wall word.

"How many of you know what your story will be about today and are ready to get started?" Hands shot up. "Off you go!"

FIG. 9–1 Alexa's story about dancing the Macarena at a party.

Ensuring Writers Have a Clear Narrative with a Beginning, Middle, and End

I PULLED UP NEXT TO COLLEEN FOR A CONFERENCE. She was intent on adding details to her amazing drawings (see Figure 9–1). She almost did not notice that I was there to work with her. I said, "Colleen, what are you working on right now?" She looked up a little reluctantly. She said, "I have a great story here, and so I want

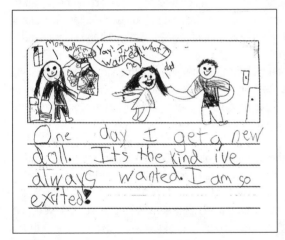

FIG. 9–2 Colleen's doll story

"Writers, it's time to take a small break from our writing and meet with our partners again. Can you please put your pencils and markers down and look up at me for a minute?" I waited until I had their attention. "We are going to use our partners, right now, to help make sure that we are including storytelling words in our writing, okay? Partner 1 will start. Try telling the story of your pictures to your partner using your best storytelling words. Try to capture a special word or two from your sharing, and then add those words into your story. Partner 2, it's your job to listen carefully and help your partner find those special storytelling words. When you're done, you can switch jobs. Okay, go!" I circulated through the classroom, listening in. When I noticed the first partner finishing up, I reminded the students to switch roles. Notice the storytelling language in Figure 9–2.

to make sure that my pictures are great, too!" I said, "Can we read it?" "Sure." Then she read:

> One day I get a new doll. Its the kind I've always wanted. I am so excited.
>
> Her birthday is this month! I can't wait to celebrate it!
>
> Her personality is super careful. Her favorite drink is orange juice. I poured the orange juice from my teapot.
>
> She even has a pet. It is a pet bear. My brother loves it!

When Colleen finished reading, I agreed with her. I thought her writing was great. What I also thought was that it was not a story. Given that this was halfway through a unit teaching kids to write true *stories*, I decided that it was probably important to make sure she knew how to do just that. Before I began to teach, I jotted Colleen's strengths in my conferring notes. I wrote: *detailed*, storytelling pictures, and *meaningful story ideas*. I also jotted her needs: *Confuses narrative and non-narrative* and *doesn't include picture details in words*.

After jotting my notes, I continued. "Colleen, when I read the words you wrote, I do not hear a story. Instead, what I hear is all about your favorite doll. That kind of writing is writing that teaches, and we did that kind of writing during the last unit."

I turned to the second page. "Like this page. The picture looks like it could be a plan to tell the story of your doll's birthday celebration. But, instead you wrote some facts about your doll. Fact #1—Her birthday is this month. Fact #2—I can't wait to celebrate it.

"Story writing involves a person who does something in some kind of order, usually involving a beginning and a middle and an end. Your story has a person, you, and in the pictures, it looks like there is a story there. It looks like you have a birthday party for your doll. Is that right?" I asked.

After tracing her finger over the doll in the picture, Colleen answered, "Yeah. This is a picture of her birthday party. Do you see the calendar with the birthday marked?"

"I do. I love knowing that detail that your doll's birthday is so important to you that you even mark it on the calendar! That is some kind of love you have for your doll! Do you see what I mean about how you still have yet to tell the *story* of the party, telling what happened first, next, and then last?

"How about if we try to tell the story together now?" She nodded. I continued, "Colleen, look at the picture that you drew on the page, and use it to help you remember how your doll's birthday party started."

Colleen said, "It was time for my doll's party. It was on the calendar."

"Then . . ."

"I gave my doll some cake."

Soon Colleen was telling a long, detailed story that ends with, "And then, we sang happy birthday to her."

I smiled and said, "Yes! Now you have a story. You also have a way for you to find the important story ideas from your life. You now know that sometimes you have an idea for a story, but you want to teach me facts instead of spin a tale about that day. What you can do now, when you need to tell a story, is to make sure you have a person who does something. Then you just need to tell that story with a beginning, middle, and end."

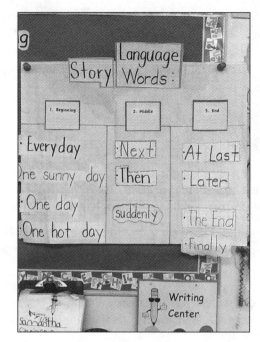

FIG. 9–3 "Story Language Words" chart

Using More Specific Words in Our Writing

Highlight a student who tried out a new strategy in his or her writing. In this case, celebrate a student who used specific words for the people, places, and things in his or her story and for the actions.

"You guys have been writing with your words and your voice. As I worked with you all today, I could almost hear you talking to me as I read your writing on the page. A story is so much better when it is told in the voice of a person you know.

"I want to show you one more thing that I found myself teaching Shavon today. When it comes to collecting words, when it comes to figuring out which words to pay attention to, there are really two kinds of words that really matter— people-place-thing words and action words.

"You guys have your own ways of *talking* about the people and places and things in your life and so you need to make sure you *write* using those words, too. In Shavon's story about playing at the beach, he wrote, 'We made a house and put on our men.' But, when he told me the story from his pictures he said, 'We built a castle and put our Spidermen on it.' The specific things—castle and Spidermen—really matter. Those words make the story more Shavon.

"The action words also matter. At first Shavon had the word *made*. It was the word for what he did, his action, and it was a word he knew in a snap. But, when he told his story he said the word 'built.' He decided to change his action word from *made* to *built*.

"When you are trying to write in your own words, you can pay special attention to the people-place-thing words and the action words. When these two kinds of words more closely match the way you talk, then your true stories are more enjoyable."

Session 10

Using Reading Partnerships to Support More Conventional Writing

THIS SESSION UPS THE ANTE while also providing dramatic new support. For a while now, children have tried—with the help of tools such as the word wall and the vowel chart—to write true stories in such a way that *we* can read their writing. Now we'll ask them to write so that *their peers* can read their stories. This is a bigger challenge; it's easier for an adult to figure out what the child was trying to say than for another child.

As has been the case throughout this unit, the same expectations that will raise the bar can also overwhelm students, so again, you will need to be judicious. When some children realize that although their teacher was pretty good at deciphering parts of their writing, their classmates really can't decode their invented spellings, this can be a cause for some dismay. But there are tremendous gains to be had from nudging children to persevere at the job of writing so their classmates can read their writing. Imagine the hard, constructive work of a child adding more and more letters to a word, then passing it to his friend saying, "*Now* can you read it?" Perhaps in the end, the writer resorts to saying, "I'm trying to say . . ." and then asking his or her friend, "Will you help me write it so you can read it?"

Today and for the remaining days of this unit we suggest you bring your *reading* partnerships into your writing workshop. First, this sends the message that a big part of writing is reading one's writing, and that youngsters need to draw on what they know about reading when attempting to read their own and each other's writing. Touch the words, get their mouths ready, think, "What would make sense?" and so forth.

There are other more practical reasons to rely on reading partnerships today and during the upcoming stretch of time. Presumably, those reading partnerships are ability-based (and the writing ones will not have been). When a main objective is for children to be able to read their partner's writing, this is more apt to happen if the more proficient readers and writers are working together. They'll produce longer texts that require higher levels of reading knowledge.

But the most important value is that by relying on reading partnerships, you dramatize that reading is reading, whether one is reading a Joy Cowley book or reading a classmate's book, and always, children need to draw on all they know about reading in order to do this important work.

IN THIS SESSION, you'll teach students that writers use a partner as a tool to help make writing more readable.

GETTING READY

✔ Student writing folders (see Connection and Active Engagement)

✔ An example of an independent reading book from Reading Workshop; in this case we use a Joy Cowley book (see Teaching)

✔ Teacher-created writing sample (see Teaching)

✔ Narrative Writing Checklist, Grades K and 1 (see Teaching)

✔ Pencils with erasers, one for each student (see Active Engagement and Share)

✔ Several books with simple text for the students to study as mentors; here we use Joy Cowley and Bill Cosby (see Mid-Workshop Teaching)

✔ Plan on a new seating arrangement in the Minilesson. Lay writing folders out in the meeting area in such a way that reading partners sit alongside each other.

COMMON CORE STATE STANDARDS: W.K.3, W.K.5, W.K.6, W.K.7, W.1.3, RFS.K.1, RFS.K.2, RFS.K.3, SL.K.1, SL.K.2, SL.K.3, SL.K.6, L.K.1, L.K.2

Using Reading Partnerships to Support More Conventional Writing

CONNECTION

Orchestrate things so kids are sitting with reading (not writing) partners, then explain that you are upping the ante by asking them to write so *kids* (not *teachers*) can read their writing.

After laying children's writing folders out on the carpet, I called the children to the meeting area. "Writers, when you come to the meeting area today, you will see that your folders are laid out in a new sort of a way. Will you find your folder and sit on it? When you are all here and looking at me, ready to listen, we will get started." Children came, finding their folders arranged so that they sat with a partner.

"Writers, last night I took your stories home, and I sat with a cup of tea, wrapped in a nice blanket, reading over your stories. I read about Camila meeting a ladybug and about how Gustavo invented a new game with chalk and a water gun. I snuggled even further down into my blanket to enjoy Brian's story about losing a tooth, and I laughed while reading Colleen's story about how her play date thought her bed was too girly! The amazing thing was that I could read most of what you'd written. It has only been a few weeks since you started working to make your writing so that *I* could read it—and for the most part, you've pulled that off.

"So today I am going to suggest a new and harder goal for you—you ready? I am wondering if, for the next week, you would be willing to work like crazy to make your writing *so easy* to read that not just teachers but also *kids* can read your writing. You have to put more letters in, and more spaces, and more punctuation, and you need even more helpful letters if you are writing for kids, because teachers have gone to college to learn to figure out what a kid's paper says. Kids need for your writing to be a lot like Dr. Seuss's or Mo Willems's writing.

"What this means is that you'll write new stories every day, pretty much, and then at the end of the day, you can take your story to one kid, and another, and say, 'Can you read this?' and then you can watch and see how you did. Can that kid read your writing? If so, thumbs up. Or is the writing still hard to read? If so," and I made a muscle, "you've got more work to do."

Sometimes we think very hard about the words we're going to say in a minilesson but overlook the importance of social organizations. By seating children in their reading partnerships, you make convey to children that although this is writing time, and they'll be working with partners to read. This time, the texts your children read will be their own.

Set up the teaching point, and create cohesion in the bend of the unit, by suggesting that partners can be used as a kind of tool to get the job done.

"But the good news is that I am going to give you a new kind of tool to help you get this big job done. So far, I have given you checklists and vowel charts and word walls—but today, I want to tell you that you can use your partner as a Power Tool."

❋ Name the teaching point.

"Today I want to teach you that when writers are working to make their writing more readable, it helps if the writer has a partner who works with the writer—like a team—to get the job done."

TEACHING

Explain that kids are sitting beside reading partners because at the end of writing time, they'll read as if it is reading time, only with their books and magic pencils in hand, upping the readability.

"Writers, I'm sure you have noticed that you are now sitting beside your *reading* partner. Your reading partner (not your writing partner) will be your partner during writing workshop for the next bunch of days. So reading partners, what I am going to suggest is that every day, at the end of writing time, you get your books out," and I held a reading book by Joy Cowley, "just like you do during reading time, and put the book between the two of you," I enacted a reading partnership, to illustrate, using the Joy Cowley book, "and you read together." I pointed under some words, imitating the reading work that children do. "*Only*, here's the thing: the books that you will be reading at the end of every day's writing workshop won't be books written by Joy Cowley and Bill Martin and Bill Cosby. They will be written by you," and I pointed to one writer, "and you," and again I pointed, "and you—by all of you.

"In a few days, you will be doing this reading to test out all the books that all the kids in this class are writing and see if you *can* read them.

"But for today and the next few days, when you do this reading, you will do it with your magic pencils, and both you and your partner will switch between reading and writing, reading and writing. Together, you will help each other make your books as readable as possible."

Demonstrate how you hope children read with their reading partners, modeling the shifts between reading and writing and the use of tools to help. Be brief and efficient.

"So guys, Zoe is going to be my partner, and we are going to show you how kids can work together to use all of our tools and to make easy to read writing—together." Shifting the story so that it was not on my legs but between the two of us, I stage whispered, "Just like during reading, we put the writing in the middle so we can both see it." Then I said, "So we both point and read. It is almost like our hands are on top of each other's. The writer reads *aloud*, the reader whisper-reads, then we switch parts."

It's incredibly important to take the content from previous days and weave it into the fabric of your minilessons.

We both reached for our magic pencils—eraser end out—to touch the words, but just before we started, I said, "Here's the thing. This is reading to make the writing easier to read. So if either one of us thinks, 'Wait, we need to check the word wall,' then we go," and I made a stop-the-traffic hand gesture," and we talk about it." Zoe and I read two pages together:

> I like to play basketball. I like to make baskets.

Then I used the hand gesture to signal "stop," and I said, "I think we gotta check the story chart because I am not sure this is a real story yet." We gestured to the Narrative Writing Checklist, and Zoe read:

> *Tells what happened first, then next, then next.*

Zoe said, "You are right. You've got to tell about one time when you played basketball."

I said, "Oops! Magic pencil!" and flipped my pencil to the writing end and started to write.

ACTIVE ENGAGEMENT

Ask reading partners to read one page of one partner's writing in the same manner, shifting between reading and writing as they help each other make the text more readable.

"Now I want you guys to try it. I know during reading time, you sit together, Partners 1 and 2, so Partner 2, take out one of your stories. Then do the work of reading together—just like you do during reading time—only be sure that this time you shift between reading and writing as you help make the story more readable. Go."

I moved among the children, noticing and, in voiceover comments, naming the behaviors that I observed. "So many magic pencils and so many eyes are linked to the words and letters. Nice. I'm seeing people work with word wall charts and vowel charts—nice."

Riley looked up and said, "I see a lot of fix-up stuff in my partner's story."

I said, in a voice loud enough for the class, "Often it is easier to help someone else fix up their writing than it is to fix up your own writing. Go to it! And don't forget to use your word wall."

LINK

Remind children that partner reading will come at the end of writing time. First they need to write the story they'll then ask partners to try to read. Scaffold to get story ideas flowing.

"Writers, I am getting ready to send you off to do your writing work. But, you are only going to read together like this *at the very end* of writing time. Before you can do that, you need to write a new story. So let's think for a second about

Teachers, notice of course that the piece of writing was deliberately written to highlight the problem we'd decided to emphasize and to get to the problem quickly. We decided to highlight an issue with the narrative craft rather than with spelling or punctuation so as to keep that aspect of this unit alive, but it also makes the level of work that is being illustrated very high. You could decide to have made a much more obvious and easy-to-repair error in your writing—misspelling the *for example. There would be lots of advantages to that choice.*

Compliments can be a way to remind children to draw on all they've learned earlier. Never underestimate their power.

what you might write about. I'll ask some questions that should make an idea for a true story pop into your mind, and when you get one in mind, signal to your partner that you've got a story idea."

Then I began supporting a chain of free association. "Think right now about something you did at home just the other day. It could be something small, like fighting with your brother over the TV remote, or your mom telling you to run or you'd be late for school.

"Think about a time you had a strong feeling recently. Maybe you were really sad. Maybe you were really glad.

"Think about the stuff you are wearing right now. What stories does that stuff bring to mind? Can you remember buying those shoes, or some other ones? Think about the stuff you like in your house. What have you done with some of that stuff?"

Dismiss writers once both partners have a story idea.

"When *both* partners have a story idea, you can zip back to your work spots and get started on your writing."

Working Deliberately to Improve the Quality of Your Conferring

ALTHOUGH YOU WILL HAVE TAUGHT A MINILESSON that suggested today is something of a turning point within the bend of the unit—and hopefully you will have inspired new levels of resolve—the truth is that the actual work that children are doing today is not different from the work they have been doing for the past week. This means that they should be fairly good at it, and you should be able to work a bit on the quality of your teaching. This write-up, then, is designed to help you work with some deliberateness to improve the level of teaching that you do during your conferences.

As mentioned in the *Guide to the Common Core Writing Workshop*, the research is really clear that when a teacher wants to accelerate students' levels of achievement, one of the best things she can do is to improve the quality and increase the quantity of the feedback she gives her students. John Hattie has done a mega-study involving literally millions of people learning a host of different things, and he found that when teachers give learners quality feedback, this makes a bigger difference than almost anything else they can do.

Quality feedback starts with the learner having a crystal clear goal that he or she is working toward. This session, and all of the teaching you have been doing all along, aims to give the class that goal, but in your conferences, you will definitely want to check in on what the writer is trying to do. If the writer produces the lingo of the class, like "I'm trying to make it so kids can read this," then you will want to get the writer to say more. Does she think the kids *can* read her story? What does she have to work on to make the story easier to read?

Different children will need to work on different things. For one, the way to make a story more readable will include more labels, each with more letters in them, and more representational and detailed pictures. For another, it will mean slowing down and hearing lots of sounds in a word. For another, the problem now is the writer doesn't progress from start to finish through a word but instead says the word repeatedly, each time tapping in to hear different sounds from any ol' place in the word. You are

going to want to help each writer understand the specific goal that he or she needs to work toward.

MID-WORKSHOP TEACHING **Learning from Mentor Texts**

"Writers. Oops, writers. I need your attention. Pencils down and eyes up here, please." I scanned the room, waiting to see that I had everyone's attention. Once I did, I continued. "One thing I forgot to point out. You guys are making books, like Joy Cowley and Bill Cosby make books." I put a book on each writer's desk. "Check those books for all sorts of tips about what writers do do—and don't do. You'll see that Bill Cosby doesn't write," and I crouched down and spoke in a wee little voice, "lowercase letter," and I rose up on my toes, speaking in a big voice, "*capital letter*," and I crouched again," "lowercase and then," I rose, "*capital* in a row. He doesn't write like this":

BeE fLeW

"Notice that in books by authors you love, most letters are lowercase and there are only some capital letters, like at the start of a sentence. You might notice other things, too, that authors do—or don't do. You can do your own investigating!"

As Students Continue Working . . .

"Remember, guys, that you will soon share your writing with your partner. You need to be writing with that partner in your mind. It is almost as if you are living toward the time when your partner will let you know if your writing actually *is* easy to read. As you write, keep asking yourself, 'Do I think my partner will be able to read this?'"

Quality feedback also involves providing positive support for any progress the learner has already made, and doing this in a way that helps the learner construct a story line of himself or herself as someone who can work hard, use strategies, and get better. You will want to help writers see that not long ago they were doing one thing, and now, with the help of hard work and strategies—look at the progress! This means that your conferences will often involve you and the writer looking back to earlier work, contrasting that work with today's effort.

And then, finally, quality feedback means you telling the writer precisely and specifically what he or she can do next to get better. Borrow from some of what you have learned to do through minilessons in order to show the writer what he or she can do next. Study how demonstration teaching tends to go and how scaffolding tends to go, because during this final part of a conference, you will often say, "Let's try that together," and then actually step forward and do a tiny bit of demonstrating. Then pause to name what you just did that you hope the writer will do. Finallly, you say—as you do in an active engagement section of a minilesson—"Why don't you try it?" Then as the writer tries whatever you have just demonstrated, you do some voicing over or provide some lean coaching to steer the writer's work without interfering in it.

If you work on these guidelines while conferring, you should find that students' progress is tangible and palpable. And here is the most important tip of all: watch that progress. If you confer to teach something, check in to see what happens as a result. And when you do that checking in to see the results, know that you are checking on yourself and the effectiveness of your teaching. If the child learns and improves—bravo to you! If not, well, then the message to you is the same message that kids will get when someone can't yet read their writing—time to roll up your sleeves and work harder.

Reading with Partners:
Is Our Writing Easier to Read?

Immediately send students into their partnerships so they can begin reading their writing together.

"Writers, I do not want to say one single word. I do not want to take up any of your precious reading time. Get together with your reading partner, and remember what you know about reading together. Don't forget to have your magic pencil with you!" I zipped my lips in a dramatic fashion and signaled for them to hurry, hurry, to read together.

As children read together, I moved among them, noticing ways in which they were working productively that I could compliment to them and sometimes to the larger group.

Reconvene the group to highlight a partnership that was working productively to make each other's writing more readable.

"As I moved around and listened in on your partnership talk, I was noticing all sorts of wonderful things happening! I want to tell you all about this, since writers—and partners, too—can learn from each other. One thing I noticed was that Grace and Shavon were using one of their Writing Power Tools, the list of 'What Makes Writing Easy to Read.' They read over the chart together and then noticed that there was a little bit of a problem on the second page. Grace was able to read the sentence that she wrote there, but you know what? Shavon wasn't! And remember, we said that it's not just important for you or me to be able to read your writing, but you want to make sure that your writing is readable so that *anyone* who sits down to read it can. So then, Shavon and Grace worked together, flipping to the writing side of the magic pencil, to make sure that the words were easier for *both* kids to read. Excellent work, partners!"

I take my tooth out.

FIG. 10–1   Grace's tooth story

I saw blood out.

I showed my tooth to mom.

Session 11

Using a Partner to Hear More Sounds in Words

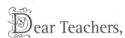ear Teachers,

Since the beginning of the school year, your students have been involved in partnerships across many curricular areas. There are a variety of reasons to get your students working one on one with their peers and a variety of ways that you can set them up to work together. As with everything else in your kindergarten classroom, it is important that you explicitly teach your students how to engage with their partners, as well as set clear expectations for what you hope they achieve.

Recently, you have made a shift in your class writing partnerships. Prior to a few sessions ago, your students were working in partnerships where it was not imperative that they be at the same ability level. Perhaps you paired them off for social or behavioral reasons. Or maybe you created a partnership that was designed to provide one writer with more support, setting them up with a more advanced writer to provide them with that scaffolding. Now, though, they are working with their reading partners during writing workshop. These partnerships are ability based, and also familiar. So although these partnerships are new for writing, you will hopefully not have to spend very much time working through behavioral and management issues.

While this session is designed to help you teach your students how to help their partners hear more sounds in the words that they are stretching out, it will be important for you to also address how one partner can support the other partner without doing the work for them. Using metaphors or silly scenarios to illustrate this point can be helpful.

MINILESSON

You may want to begin today's minilesson by reminding students that when they are working with their partners, sometimes they are slipping into a "teacher" role. And just like a teacher doesn't do all of the work for students, one partner should not be doing all of the work for the other partner. Perhaps you will want to share a story that would help your

COMMON CORE STATE STANDARDS: W.K.3, W.K.5, RFS.K.1, RFS.K.2, RFS.K.3, SL.K.1, SL.K.6, L.K.1, L.K.2

students visualize this. For example, think of the piano teacher and student. How good would the piano teacher be if she said to her student, "Play me a song," listened as the student proceeded to tap out a few notes, and then said, "Move off that bench! Let me show you how it's done!" What if the teacher then deftly played up and down the keys, with a grand flourish? How does that help the student improve?

Reminding children of how to be a positive partner will get them ready for today's teaching, in which you teach partners a way to help each other get more sounds into the words they write. Your teaching point today will not be new. After all, your students have spent weeks stretching out words, listening for the sounds, and then getting those sounds onto their paper. Today you will teach them to do this work with a partner.

To teach children how to help each other, you may want to demonstrate how to work with a partner in ways that help you write more letters per word. Select a student to be your partner. Don't forget that you can think of this demonstration as an opportunity to show your students productive partnership behaviors. Be sure you are sitting side by side, shoulder to shoulder, holding your writing between you, so you can both read it. Explain to the class that today, they will be working with their partners with the goal of getting more sounds into the words they write. They will take turns, shifting between being the writer and the teacher/reader. Have a piece of your own writing on hand, one that contains words written with invented spellings that have some obvious sounds missing. Don't go overboard with the amount of missing sounds or then it will be impossible for your student partner to read your draft. Tell the class that you will give your writing to your partner and allow him to read it. Your partner's—the teacher/reader's—job is to read your writing, and when he comes to a word that he can't read or that is missing some sounds, he will hand it back to you, pointing out the word that is hard to read. What your partner should *not* do is tell you how to spell the word or tell you what letters are missing. Your partner should just tell you which word needs to be looked at again. You can then work together to stretch out the words and listen for the sounds. But it is your job, as the writer, to cross out the word in your writing and rewrite it in the space above. After you demonstrate and name this for your teaching, you can give the students in your class the opportunity to take on the teacher/reader role with your writing, for the active engagement. You may want to have an enlarged copy of your writing, written on chart paper, so it is easier for everyone in the class to see.

Before you send students off to work with their partners, highlight the productive ways in which the teacher/reader worked. Remind them that the teacher/reader's job was not to fix the writer's writing but instead to point out to them words that they were having trouble reading. The partners could then work together to stretch out the word and listen for more sounds. But the actual writing work was to be done by the writer. After all, a good teacher doesn't do the work for their student!

CONFERRING, SMALL-GROUP WORK, AND MID-WORKSHOP TEACHING

Today you'll want to circle among the partnerships, checking on what they are doing. Be on the lookout for partners who are fixing words for the writer rather than nudging the writer to hear more sounds and write more letters. Remind them of the piano teacher, or even what *you* do when you are conferring. After all, they are now behaving as writing "teachers" within their partnerships. This is not a responsibility to be taken lightly.

You probably are noticing that the children who struggle as writers also struggle as readers. Force yourself to notice what they—your struggling writers—do independently when they write. Tell yourself that just as you do hands-off observations without rescuing your readers, so, too, you need to stop scaffolding your writers enough to take in what they can and can't do. For each struggler, decide on a few next steps. Your goal isn't perfect spelling or spacing; your goal is for each child to begin to make steady progress. These partnerships may also need more support from you. Perhaps you will pull a small group, two to three partnerships, around the table and alternate between coaching them and pulling back to watch. Remember, your goal has to be independence, no matter what level of work your students are doing.

While students are busy working, you will likely coach them with some mid-workshop voiceovers. Highlight partnerships that are working in a productive manner. Name the behaviors, so other partnerships can replicate. You can also coach students into listening carefully and being sure to record all of the sounds that they are hearing on their papers. After all, that was a major point of today's minilesson, and a strategy that your students are still working on.

SHARE

Today you can use your share session to highlight an especially effective partnership. Perhaps you will write one of the partners' sentences on chart paper, and then ask both partners to replay the way they had worked together. Name for the rest of the class what it is the partners are doing, how they are working successfully as writer and teacher/reader. Remind the students that they can and should all be working like this with their partners. Give them a round of applause, a pat on the back, for being not just wonderful writers but wonderful writing teachers as well!

Putting It Together
How to Make Readable Writing (Guided Inquiry Lesson)

IN THIS SESSION, you'll teach students that writers reflect on their past work and what they have learned in order to make plans to move forward in their writing.

GETTING READY

✓ List of "What Makes Writing Easy to Read" (see Connection)

✓ Student writing folders, full of writing from the entire unit (see Teaching and Share)

✓ Post-it notes

✓ Narrative Writing Checklist, Grades K and 1 (see Share) 🏫

T HIS SESSION COMES AT THE END of the second bend for a very important reason. This is a session that asks your kindergarten writers to use all of the strategies they have learned so far in this unit to help them make their entire folder full of writing as readable as possible. They will use their Narrative Writing Checklist to complete this task. Before the next bend begins, this session serves as a little breather, a little space, but it is not empty space. This session guides children through an inquiry of their own folders so that they can try applying what they have learned in any one session to all of the true stories that are in their folders up to this point.

How crucial it is to make space during the year for children to transfer and apply all they have learned. After all, the entire goal of a writing workshop is to teach in ways that affect youngsters' lives as writers, readers, thinkers, learners. This session, then, gestures toward recognizing that teaching for transfer is always important. You'll see that the lesson is an inquiry lesson, following a different template than that which is used more traditionally in minilessons that aim to explicitly teach the skills and strategies of proficient reading. Now you are saying to youngsters, "I'm not exactly sure how to do this work, but I bet we can work together and figure something out."

If many of your students seem to thrive under this instruction, you may want to take the template for this minilesson and see instances when you can use it across your entire day.

Just one small note about the logistics of this session: it will unfold better if you look through each child's folder (or many folders) beforehand. You will know how to better guide the class inquiry if you have a more specific and detailed understanding of what your children will be doing. The conferring write-up for this session channels your study of student work, so you may want to read that now, as you prepare to teach this session. If most of a child's folder looks like the work in Figure 12–1, you'll aim your teaching differently than if it looks like the work in Figure 12–2.

COMMON CORE STATE STANDARDS: W.K.3, W.K.5, RFS.K.1, RFS.K.2, RFS.K.3, RFS.K.4, SL.K.1, L.K.1, L.K.2

Putting It Together
How to Make Readable Writing (Guided Inquiry Lesson)

CONNECTION

Channel students to brag about what they've learned to do to make their writing easier to read.

"I am more excited than usual today. You have been really working hard for several days now to make your writing easy to read." I pointed to the "What Makes Writing Easy to Read" chart as I said this. "Each of you has been working to do these things in your writing," and I moved my hand down the chart and across my list. "Take a second right now to brag a little to the person next to you about all the different things you have been trying to make your work easier to read."

```
What Makes Writing Easy to Read
spaces ("it isn't all scrunched together")  girl
neat ("without a lot of eraser marks")  clean
pictures that help  sun
hear lots of sounds in a word  (xa) (ch)
leave spaces between words   I walked my dog.
make pictures that hold the words of the
story  ♡ Love
Use  CAPITALS at the start of a sentence
Use punctuation at the end of a sentence.
                    .!?, .!?
```

After a burst and buzz of voices that resounded with teaching points taken from the chart and from the unit, I said, "That's why I am excited today! You guys were saying that you pay attention to things like vowels, and spaces between words, and stretching words out to hear the sounds, and sight words, and that when you do all those things, your writing becomes much easier to read. That is exactly what I notice when I study the writing in your folders."

◆ COACHING

If it seems that the teaching has been a bit of a broken record, returning to the same emphases over and over—that's what it takes. The goal is to habitualize an attentiveness to conventions, and this requires repeated practice. Think about a time when you've work hard at skill development—perhaps a time when you learned to play tennis, or soccer, perhaps a time you learned a musical instrument. You no doubt recall a lot of repeated practice—and the high that came as you saw your level of proficiency increase. That's what your students are experiencing now.

Describe the differences between today's inquiry lesson and a traditional minilesson format.

"Today is the ending of the second part of the unit. Before we go on to new and even harder challenges, it can sometimes be helpful to stop and notice what you have learned to do. Sometimes writers take a break from their work to look back over all that they have done so far. I think you might do some of that now. You might try to gather up *all* your new learning and use it in all your old stories before you move on to new projects."

❖ Guided Inquiry

Name a question that will guide personal inquiries. In this case, writers will ask, "What have I learned to do that makes my writing more readable? What could I still learn that would help my writing become even *more* readable?"

TEACHING

Set up writers to reread as much of their writing as they can. Then listen in and coach.

"So, writers, let's do that work now! Would you move to the edge of the rug, bringing your writing folder with you, so that you are sitting in a rectangle and so you have space in front of you in which to spread out your work." I did some directing for those children who found sitting on the edge of the rug a complicated process.

Once everyone was settled in their new workspace, I began again, "So, the first thing you need to do is to look back through all of the writing you have done so far. Will you first just read over a piece of writing, and remember the time you were writing about?"

Coach writers in a step-by-step way to use early reading behaviors to read their writing.

I sat in the middle of the meeting area, and turned as I spoke, like the dials on the clock. "Writers, will you get your reading fingers ready, and start reading, pointing under each word. If you are not sure what a word says, check the picture and see if you can remember the story. Then work hard at figuring out what the letters might say. If you can't read one page, that's okay. Try another." As I turned slowly in the middle of the circle of folders and stories and writers, I reminded children to read with their pointer fingers. I called, "Keep reading. All your stories."

I also coached specific children, leaning on what I had learned from assessing their whole folder before this session. I said, "Liam, I want you to make sure you are paying attention to your word wall words. See here—that is a word you just know in a snap." I turned to Zoe and said, "Make sure you read your drawing if you need help holding on to your story."

If you have worked to increase the Depth-of-Knowledge level of your teaching, you will realize that you increase the level of cognitive challenge for students when you ask them to study the patterns in their previous work, noticing how their work has changed over time.

It's noteworthy to see that this unit, like many effective minilessons, is coming around full circle. Children will revisit their earlier work, this time bringing their new knowledge and skills.

Once writers have read most of their work, channel them to notice specific things they have done that make their writing readable.

"Okay, writers, so now will you investigate the big questions. What have you done that makes your writing more readable? What do you still need to work on doing? Look closely at just one page—any page—and think, 'What did I do to help me read this page?' Put a Post-it beside things you notice that you have done that really work for you."

Coach into children's work, prompting them to find evidence of the items on class charts and to talk with partners about what they notice.

As children worked, I voiced over, prompting them to look at the chart to see if they had made their writing more readable, such as spaces between words, vowels in the middles of words, capital letters at the beginning, word wall words, and so on.

After a few minutes, I said, "Writers, turn and talk to each other about some of the things you notice yourself doing that have made your writing readable."

Next, ask students to look at the same pages, noticing things they could still do.

"Writers, next, think about what you can do to make your writing more readable. I want to suggest one thing that I think is important. I've been noticing that you fairly often have abandoned your stories halfway. Will you go through your folder and make a pile of work that is done and a pile of work that is not done.

"If there is a part of your writing where you can't read it, think about what the problem might be. Have you forgotten to leave spaces or not spelled words with enough sounds? Mark places where you notice the page needs work."

I again circled, coaching children to leave Post-it reminders on places where they could do some work. I asked writers to be sure to notice pieces that weren't done, and to mark those. After a few minutes of marking their pages, I said, "Guys, I am going to stop you now. I know you have not put Post-it notes in every story yet, but I think you have done enough to get started."

With a messy stack of stories in front of her, Riley said, "I have a *lot* of work to do!" and she smiled.

LINK

Rally your kids to go back to their tables and begin to work, using the self-assessment they just did to make plans for moving forward.

I smiled and nodded. "Gather up your pile and your folder and head to your table, with your plans for work that will make your whole folder easier to read. Remember that this is what writers do. Writers take a breather to look back over the work they have done so far and to think about what's working well and what they need to do next."

Famous Writers Use Periods to Tell Readers When to Stop

Teaching Children to Use Periods

YOU'LL WANT TO RESEARCH by observing and interviewing students, to understand what each is trying to do as a writer who aims to make her writing easier to read. In one case, I noticed Camilla writing a sentence or two at the bottom of each page, without using punctuation. Watching Camilla was helpful because it soon became clear that although she didn't use any punctuation at all, she did segment her writing into sentences, dictating what was clearly one sentence at a time to herself and taking a little rest from writing whenever a sentence was complete.

I decided to demonstrate to Camilla how writers use end punctuation to help people read their writing, by reading both a published book and Camilla's own writing with and without the help of punctuation.

"Camilla," I began, setting her up to learn from the demonstration by naming what I aimed to do, "there is one thing you could do to make your writing much easier for me to read. It is something that grown-up famous authors do." Then I opened a book she'd been reading by Bill Martin and pointed to the punctuation.

"I want to show you how, when I am reading, these periods help me know when to stop. The periods are like red lights when I am driving. They say, 'Stop for a second; take a breath!' Let me show you."

I began to read, placing my finger under each word and, in due course, under each period. I paused dramatically for each of the periods and took an exaggerated breath. Camilla giggled. Then I helped her get started doing what I had demonstrated. "You try it—let the periods make you stop," I said. Camilla then reread the same page, pausing just as dramatically for the periods. Next I demonstrated how it would feel to read writing with no end punctuation.

"Now watch what happens if we pretend that Bill Martin doesn't have periods in his writing," I said. "It would go like this." I reread the same text in a silly words-falling-all-over-each-other fashion. "What I noticed when I tried to read your writing (other than

MID-WORKSHOP TEACHING Moving Pieces to the Finished Side of Your Folder When They Are Complete

"Writers, look up for a minute please. We are about halfway through our workshop time for today, and I just want to make sure that you are taking the Post-it notes out of your stories as you do the work of making that place more readable. And, once you have finished making a particular story more readable, if it is a finished story with all the pictures drawn and the words written, then you can put that story on the finished side of your folder. If you are finished making your stories stronger, then you will of course go back to thinking and drawing and writing new readable stories."

As Students Continue Working . . .

"Don't forget, if you had stories that you started and did not finish, please try to finish those stories today. Make sure you don't just turn to the blank page and try to fill it in. First reread the pages you have already written so that you can remember which parts of the story you have told so far. Then you are ready to work on telling the rest of the story."

the great spelling) is that you forgot to put periods in. When I first read this page, I read it like this," I said, and I reenacted a silly unpunctuated reading of her text.

Again, I helped Camilla get started by asking her to read her writing, listening for where periods should go and adding them: "Will you read your writing the way it is *supposed* to go?" I asked. She did, pausing dramatically at the end of each sentence and smiling up at me mischievously.

Next, taking Camilla back to the beginning of the process, I helped her get started putting periods into her sentences. "So now, Camilla, pay close attention to where you need to add periods to your own work so it doesn't just keep going and going without giving the reader a place to stop and breathe! Let's get started adding periods together."

We did a bit of this work together, then Camilla continued rereading and adding punctuation. She added too many periods, sometimes using a period when in fact a comma would have been called for, but I let this go. Instead, I named the new work she had done as a writer and reminded her to do this often in future writing, setting her up to continue working. As she added a period, I said, "That's it. You are doing it just like Bill Martin! What you are doing is perfect. Keep doing this forever and forever."

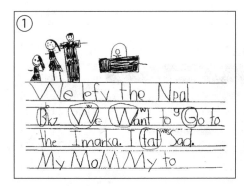

We left the Nepal because we want to go to the America. I was sad. My mommy too.

FIG. 12–1   Niki's Nepal story

Plane took off. We thinking we are coming back.

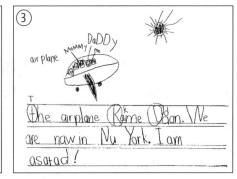

The airplane came down. We are now in New York. I am excited!

My family is roller skating.

FIG. 12–2   Jaevaughn's roller-skating story

My family went to the store.

My family goes to the park.

Self-Assessment and Goal Setting

Guide children to self-assess their growth as writers.

"Writers, you have been working *so hard* lately to make your writing easy to read. In fact, right now, let's all take a quick bow in appreciation for all the hard work that you have done." There was much giggling and cheering as the children bowed, proud of all they had accomplished.

"I want to end our writing workshop today by letting you in on a little writing secret. You ready to hear it?" The children eagerly nodded their heads. "Okay, lean in close. Here it is—writers are *always* looking to get better. And one way that writers do this is by reading over writing they have already done, and saying things like, "Yeah, I did a really good job of this" or "Whoa, I really should work on this." I thought it would be a great idea for us to do that today. So right now, take out a piece of writing from the 'Finished' side of your folder." I waited while the students rifled through their pieces.

"Fantastic. Now close your folders and sit right on top of them. Only one story should be in your hands. Okay, let's remember, this checklist is really just a list of the things that we've been learning about, the things that writers do to make their writing easy to read. Now, I'm going to read it again, and this time, I want to you look over your writing as I do. Give a thumbs up if yes, you've already done this in this piece. If you give a thumbs up saying yes, you have done that, please point to the evidence in the piece." Then I addded, "Give a thumbs down if you haven't yet done something."

I read through the checklist, giving the children the opportunity to assess their writing as I read. "Thumbs down should really be muscles up, because this is where you have good work to do."

Narrative Writing Checklist

	Kindergarten	NOT YET	STARTING TO	YES!	Grade 1	NOT YET	STARTING TO	YES!
	Structure				**Structure**			
Overall	I told, drew, and wrote a whole story.	☐	☐	☐	I wrote about when I did something.	☐	☐	☐
Lead	I had a page that showed what happened first.	☐	☐	☐	I tried to make a beginning for my story.	☐	☐	☐
Transitions	I put my pages in order.	☐	☐	☐	I put my pages in order. I used words such as *and* and *then, so*.	☐	☐	☐
Ending	I had a page that showed what happened last in my story.	☐	☐	☐	I found a way to end my story.	☐	☐	☐
Organization	My story had a page for the beginning, a page for the middle, and a page for the end.	☐	☐	☐	I wrote my story across three or more pages.	☐	☐	☐
	Development				**Development**			
Elaboration	My story indicated who was there, what they did, and how the characters felt.	☐	☐	☐	I put the picture from my mind onto the page. I had details in pictures and words.	☐	☐	☐
Craft	I drew and wrote some details about what happened.	☐	☐	☐	I used labels and words to give details.	☐	☐	☐
	Language Conventions				**Language Conventions**			
Spelling	I could read my writing.	☐	☐	☐	I used all I knew about words and chunks of words (*at, op, it*, etc.) to help me spell.	☐	☐	☐
	I wrote a letter for the sounds I heard.	☐	☐	☐	I spelled all the word wall words right and used the word wall to help me spell other words.	☐	☐	☐
	I used the word wall to help me spell.	☐	☐	☐		☐	☐	☐

The Narrative Writing Checklist, Grades K and 1 can be found on the CD-ROM.

Writers Search Their Mental and Drawn Pictures to Make Their Stories Better

IN THIS SESSION, you'll invite your writers to make the pieces they already wrote in the first part of this unit even more amazing by revising using their own pictures in their heads and on paper.

GETTING READY

✔ Class set of revision pens, in a different color from original writing (see Teaching)

✔ Draft of story that can be used to model revision strategy, preferably a shared moment with class, a purple marker, and an easel (see Teaching)

✔ Drawn picture of moment from story (see Active Engagement)

✔ Student writing folders (see Share)

T HIS BEND IS REALLY ABOUT IMPROVING the quality of your children's storytelling. While the first two bends of this unit were mostly about improving the conventions and mechanics of their writing, this bend focuses on making their stories clearer and more fun to read.

Though this bend focuses on the revision stage of the writing process, your writers will not only be going back to previously written pieces. The revision strategies you teach in this bend will also be incorporated in new stories that children will continue to write.

As a part of your revision work, you'll teach kids to reread their writing, thinking about ways to make it even better. For writers who are still labeling, you'll want to channel them to ask, "Have I labeled enough?" or "Do the most important things have a label?" Then, too, you can teach writers to compare their pieces with the class exemplar, asking, "What's in this piece that I can put in my piece?" As writers do this kind of comparison work, they might say things like, "Our class piece has two sentences on a page. I think I want to do that, too!" Although you have asked writers to do this revision work that aligns with the Common Core State Standards (W.K.5) throughout the unit, this bend and this session in particular will demonstrate the growth your writers have made.

For this session and the next session, you will entice your writers to use revision strategies on already-written stories. However, as the bend continues, your kindergartners can practice revision on new pieces, too.

COMMON CORE STATE STANDARDS: W.K.3, W.1.3, RL.K.1, RL.K.2, SL.K.1, SL.K.4, SL.K.6, L.K.1, L.K.2

Writers Search Their Mental and Drawn Pictures to Make Their Stories Better

CONNECTION

Celebrate the children's writing so far in the unit. Tell the children that when writers really love their writing, they revise that writing.

"Writers, in my family, we have a few stories we love to tell—and we tell them over and over, just for fun. One is a story about the time my sister got lost. We tell that at Thanksgiving, and we tell it on long car rides. We love the story so much that we retell it a lot. And here's the thing—each time we retell that story, we revise it. We jazz it up a bit.

"I'm telling you this because I want to talk to you about what writers do when they love a story. When writers think, 'This is a great story that I've written'—they revise it."

❖ **Name the teaching point.**

"Today I want to teach you—remind you, really—that writers revise stories, just like you revise Lego buildings or clay creations. When a writer likes his or her story, the writer returns to it, thinking, 'How can I make this *even better*?' One way writers revise is they picture what happened in their mind (and sometimes by making a drawing) and then put what they picture onto the page."

TEACHING

Demonstrate how you begin to revise, accentuating the techniques you want your students to use: rereading the pictures and the words, envisioning one's subject, and asking, "How could I make this better?"

"When I want to revise, I first find a story I like, a story that is worth making really special," I said, leafing through the finished section of my folder. "I'm going to revise this story," I said, pulling one from the stack. "Notice what I do because soon you'll be asked to revise writing you especially like as well.

"First, I reread, and as I do this, I am thinking, 'This story is going to go in the library. Hundreds of people will read it. How can I make this even better?'" Shifting from the role of teacher to that of writer, I turned to a narrative I'd written during the previous unit. Turning the pages of my story, I muttered, "Picture this as a book in the library." I reread the story on the chart paper. "This is about a time you'll all remember. Will you help me picture what happened so we can add details from the picture into the story?" Then I turn to the text—an enlarged version was on chart paper—and I read this:

> It was morning meeting.
>
> We were counting the days of school with straws.
>
> Suddenly, someone said, "What is that smell?"
>
> I said, "Everyone check your shoes!"

Samantha raised her hand. "I remember that. We all checked our shoes for poop!" The class began to laugh uproariously. (It was *poop* after all.) I laughed a little too. "Let me try to remember that, to picture it." I closed my eyes for a few seconds and said, after a pause and some nodding, I said, "I can see it now. We were all here, checking our shoes, and people were calling, 'Not me. Nothing on mine.'"

When you revise, name the replicable strategy you use. Remind writers that they can use this strategy (in this case, envisioning the moment to add on) often.

"You are helping me realize I should add 'We all checked the bottom of our shoes. Kids were calling, "It's not me. Nothing on my shoes."'" I pointed to show where those words would soon be added.

> It was morning meeting.
>
> We were counting the days of school with straws.
>
> Suddenly, someone said, "What is that smell?"
>
> Ms. Louis said, "Everyone check your shoes!"
>
> **We all checked the bottom of our shoes.**
>
> **Kids were calling, "It's not me. Nothing on my shoes."**

"We remember what happened exactly and then we reread and think, 'What could I add?'"

Debrief in ways that accentuate the transferable process.

Then I said, "Writers do this a lot—we picture more, then we add more, helping readers picture what happened."

ACTIVE ENGAGEMENT

Ask the children to join you in thinking about how you can continue to revise your story.

"Writers, when you want to picture the story and to put that picture onto the page, you can go back to the picture in your mind—or the one on paper. For now, can you go back to the picture on our paper and search through that picture (as I said this, I traced my finger slowly around the sketch, pausing as I came to new items on it) to see if there are parts of the story we remembered to draw but forgot to write. Move your eyes—just like I am moving my finger—to all of the parts of the picture as you do this searching. I'll reread the story again, and then you can tell your partner your ideas for revision."

As the partners talked about their ideas for revision, I listened in on what they said.

Brian: "Look at the picture. The rug is dirty."

Joey: "With poop. She should add that."

Riley: "See her face. She looks upset."

Shavon: "That's 'cause she had poop on her shoes. She needs to put that."

Reconvene the class, and repeat something you heard a child say to her partner. Show children how you can revise based on the overheard suggestions. Then elicit another suggestion (or two) for revision.

"I heard lots of suggestions. Brian and Joey said that when they looked at the rug in the picture it was dirty with poop. I think we *definitely* should add that. I'll add it right here at the end of the story. Does anyone else have something we should add? Kevin? All eyes on Kevin."

Kevin said, "You should say that you were sad to find poop on your shoe." When I gestured to add this onto the end of the story, he added, "That part goes before we saw the dirt on the rug."

Show children how you add their suggested revisions. Name the specific tools you use (carets, inserts) to add on to your draft.

"Good. That is another thing writers do. They think about exactly where their revision should go. Let me reread what we have so far and think about where our two ideas should go." I reread the story. "So, I think I will use a caret (as I drew one) to insert a passage." I added, "I was sad to find poop on my shoe" before the last sentence. "Now let me reread the whole thing again."

> It was morning meeting.
>
> We were counting the days of school with straws.
>
> Suddenly, someone said, "What is that smell?"
>
> Our teacher said, "Everyone check your shoes!"

Revision *means, quite literally, "to see again,"* re-vision. *This strategy engaged children quite literally in the act of seen again. It's almost as if the drawing serves as a writer's To-Do list.*

Engagement matters tremendously. If you have to resort to stories about poop to keep everyone enthralled, go for it!

Notice that throughout the teaching and active engagement sections of minilessons, we continue to tuck in added tips, pointers, lessons. It can't be that the only content worth teaching is contained in the teaching point—or why would anyone listen beyond that? Here, we're teaching kids to consider the placement of their revisions.

We all checked the bottom of our shoes.

Kids were calling, "It's not me. Nothing on my shoes."

Our teacher was sad to find poop on her shoe.

We also saw poop on the rug.

LINK

Summarize the revision strategies you've taught. Ask the children to reread their "finished" stories and to think about what they could add to make them better.

"Today we learned that writers make the stories they like better. One way to do this is to picture the story—and then put that picture into words. We can picture the story in our minds, and add the words for what we see in our minds, or we can search the picture we drew, looking for parts we remembered to draw but forgot to write."

"So, today we'll begin this next part of our unit by doing what real writers do. You'll have a chance to go to the finished side of your writing folder. Even before you leave the rug, would you get a finished story that you love from your folder and reread it, like we reread our 'poop on the rug' story? As you do so, think about how you could revise your story. Use the picture in your mind or the picture on your page to help you add words that will make your story even more amazing."

Often the link ends with you sharing a repertoire of work that writers can draw upon. Because this is the start of a new bend, there are few choices to offer.

After a few minutes, ask the children who continued to reread their writing. Send off those who are with a purple revision pen, and keep the small group that needs more support on the rug.

"If you have an idea for how you could revise your writing, give me a thumbs up." As children begin to raise their hands, I explained that they'd be given purple revision pens to do this work. "Purple is the color of royalty, and I thought it was the perfect color for such noble work." I ceremoniously handed each child a purple revision pen as they headed back to their seats.

I'm making it as likely as possible that children will be able to get started revising up a storm.

There were still several children who continued to reread their writing, so I said, "You guys don't have any idea for revision?" They all nodded. I smiled and said, "Good. Let's have a quick small group here to help you."

Ask members of the small group to help each other revise. Coach into their work.

"Will you two work together, and you two? Read your pieces to each other. Listeners, your job will be to just listen and pay attention. Writers, if you remember something as you read that you did not write, take this purple pen and just get it down on the page. Or writers, if you find something in the pictures that you did not write with words, again use that purple pen. Listeners, make sure you help your partner capture their revisions."

I sometimes end a minilesson, especially a particularly critical one, by asking kids who have no idea what to do, to stay on the rug. I then work with them for five minutes or so to get the work I just taught going a little bit. This kind of end-of-the-minilesson small group often gives me insight into the kinds of mid-workshop teaching points that could help other children as they write.

Celebrating the Revisions Your Writers Have Made

AS YOU MOVE OUT INTO YOUR CLASS TODAY, notice, name, and cheer for any attempts to revise. The purple pen will help you spot those revisions more quickly.

You will probably have the urge, upon reading some of the purple writing, to tell your writers what they could have done to make their writing much better. In some cases, you might even feel like your idea for how you'd have improved the story is so good that you are tempted to take that purple pen and write your words right there on the page. Don't do it!

However, you will want to pay attention to how your ideas for revision differ from those of your kindergarten children. Try to name specifically what your kindergarten writers do when they revise. Then try to name specifically what you wish they were doing in the name of revision. Then, instead of asking a series of questions to get your writers to make the revisions you'd like to see, try to turn what you do into a strategy that your writers can use on their own again and again. Think of a strategy as a few steps that can help a child do something to their writing. For example, I suggested to Brian that he needed to not only picture the event, adding in what he remembers seeing, but also add in the things

---

MID-WORKSHOP TEACHING   Revising Drawings to Elaborate Stories

"Guys, would you look up for a second?" I waited for eyes up and writing utensils down. "I just wanted to show you what Lilly just did to her story because I think she has just discovered one more way to make her story and all of your stories even better.

"When Lilly was rereading her story, searching her drawing and thinking about what she could add, she realized that her drawing was missing something that was in her memory. So, she added that part to her drawing. Now she is working on adding the words that tell about her addition to her picture.

"Lilly's story was about egg hunting. She wrote about how she had collected so many eggs. But, see here?" I held up the page and pointed to a drawing of Lilly holding a basket filled with eggs. "When Lilly looked at the picture of her holding her basket, she realized she needed to add a second basket. See the purple pen where she drew another basket in her other hand?

"The cool thing about purple pen in the drawing is that it helps you remember to add purple pen to the words, too."

As Students Continue Working . . .

"Hey writers. I see some of you just sitting there like you are done writing for the day. Don't forget that you can add on to each page of your story. Think of re-reading and then using your purple pen as a second chance to tell your story in an even better way."

"And, remember, you can go to the other stories in your folder and do the same revision work on them, too!"

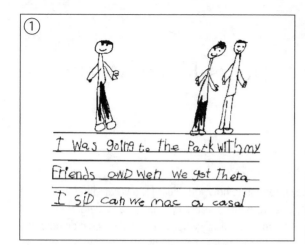

① I was going to the Park with my Friends and wen We got Theta I sid can we mac a casal

② We got in the Park We Bild a caslu my Friends Put The SPitrmen in the caslw

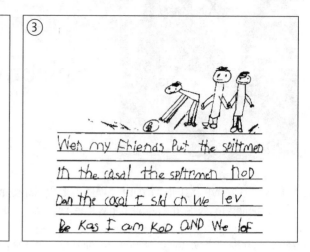

③ Wen my Fhiends Put the spitmen in the casal the spitmen nod Dan the casal I sid cn we lev Be kas I am kod aND We lof

I was going to the park with my friends and when we got there. **I said. "Can we make a castle?"**

We got in the park. We built a castle. My friends put the Spidermen in the castle.

When my friends put the Spidermen in the castle, the Spidermen knocked down the castle. **I said, "Can we leave because I am cold?"** And we left.

FIG. 13–1 Brian's revisions are in bold

he remembered hearing, saying. His two major revisions revolve around added dialogue (see Figure 13–1). If you teach one child to add not only what he sees but also what he hears, you will probably want to share that instruction with the small group at his table. You reap more benefits from a conference if you then say to the other children, "Can I stop you? Brian just came up with a terrific idea that some of you might want to try as well." Then proceed to use the one child's work to illustrate the strategy.

If a youngster rereads to think about the missing parts, and then adds in those parts—presto! You have another small group. If a youngster uses descriptive details to help readers picture whatever is getting added, or tries telling someone the whole story of the picture as a way to prime the pump again, you'll have strategies to share with others.

Although you can nudge children to get started using strategies you teach, you'll above all want to see what they've done on their own. Tell yourself, as Byrd Baylor says, that you are the one who is "in charge of celebration." If you work at it, you should be able to find reasons to celebrate. Have your writers reread? Used a caret? Added new paper? Assessed their own work? If they've done any of this, they are on a path that deserves your support. If your writers independently initiate a process of rereading and revising, this represents progress, regardless of whether the resulting products have improved. Any work with the purple pen can represent progress because your writers could be beginning a new writing habit. Remember how hard it is for you to return to and to revise work you've completed, and be ready to celebrate. Adding marginal stars can go a long way.

Celebrating Revision

Gather your students in the meeting area with their writing folders. Prepare them to share with their partners an example of the revision work they tried today.

Calling the children back to the meeting area, I said, "Bring your writing folders with you this time, and sit on them so they're not in your way as we get going. Sit next to your writing partners."

When everyone had parked on a folder, I said, "You know what was so cool about today? When I looked around the classroom, *every single one of you* was revising. I saw purple pens adding on important details to every story! I saw each of you using the pictures you'd drawn to help you add on to the words, and I saw you looking around in your memories to remember how your stories actually went and adding new things in that way, too! Revising is fun, right?

"*But,* I want to remind you about something really important: revision is about making your stories better, not just about using an awesome purple pen. Make sure you're adding important details that make your story better."

Channel students to share not just *what* they added with the purple revision pen but also how their story is better.

"Here's what we're going to do next. I'm going to ask you, when I'm done talking, to take out a piece that you revised today. You are going to find one place where you used your purple revision pen. Then you are going to tell your partner whether the section you added using the purple pen has made your writing better. You might say something like, 'I used purple pen here, and my writing is better now because readers really know now where I was when this story happened.' Or, you might say, 'My story is better because now you know who was with me.'

"So right now, take a minute to look through your folder and choose the one piece you want to share with your partner. Make sure it's a piece that you revised with purple pen. When you've chosen your piece, put it in your lap and look up." I waited until all eyes were on me, gently touching a couple of students who were getting distracted by their papers and hurrying them along.

"Great. Now turn so that you and your partner are looking at each other, and take turns sharing a place where you revised today. Don't forget to tell your partner about *how* your piece is better because of your purple pen." As the writers began, I circulated, helping students who needed support explaining the thinking behind their revision choices.

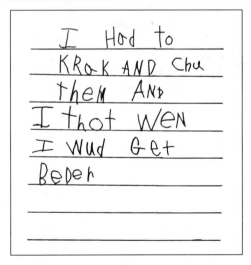

FIG. 13–2 After rereading her story (p. 1), Emma added a second page and marked its insertion point on the first page with a "secret code" (see box).

Writers Use Flaps to Make Better Stories

IN THIS SESSION, you'll teach children to use tools and techniques to insert material into many different places of their drafts. These tools should make your writers story builders.

GETTING READY

✔ Sample of student writing that can illustrate using a flap for additional space (see Teaching)

✔ Draft of class story used in Session 13 (see Teaching)

✔ Revision flaps, precut (see Teaching and Active Engagement)

✔ Revision folders (see Active Engagement)

✔ "Toolboxes" containing revision pens, scissors, staplers, and tape (see Active Engagement)

T HIS SESSION IS ALL ABOUT MAKING A MESS. Just like the gap-toothed smiles of your kindergarten students can be evidence of growth, so, too, carets, cross-outs, flaps, Post-it notes, and extra pages can be evidence of writing growth.

In this session, you'll give children tools—flaps for added text, carets, arrows, new pages—to make drafts malleable. They'll learn to insert new material into the middle of their drafts, not just at the end. In the previous session, in the name of revision, many children just added to the endings of their pages and stories, presumably because there were blank lines at the endings of pages and stories. Today you'll help children imagine ways to revise within a page, and you'll channel them to think not only about what to add to a draft, but also about where to make these revisions. Otherwise, revision can lead to chaotic narratives. Today's session helps children find the right place to insert new material.

Although this minilesson will be a step in the right direction, many of the revisions that your writers make will still not strengthen their writing. Remember, your job right now is to recruit children's enthusiastic participation in revision, so don't feel frustrated when their revisions make their pieces worse. Celebrate the fact that your writers revise and know that we'll continue improving those revisions.

You may find that some writers produce little if they are channeled to spend all their writing time revising finished drafts. In that case, channel these children to start new drafts, revising as they go.

COMMON CORE STATE STANDARDS: W.K.3, W.K.5, W.1.5, RL.K.3, SL.K.1, SL.K.2, SL.K.5, SL.K.6, L.K.1, L.K.2

Writers Use Flaps to Make Better Stories

CONNECTION

Tell the children that writers use tools to revise, and today you'll introduce some.

Once the writers had gathered at my feet, sitting in their rug spots, I began. "I've had some workmen in my kitchen lately, doing some work to make it a better kitchen. I was passing through the kitchen, and I noticed that the workmen each wear those carpenter belts. Have you ever seen them, belts that hold their tools?" I stood up and pretended to put on a belt. "They wear those tool belts because they have work to do, and they need tools to help them get that work done.

"Well, yesterday while I watched you revise, I realized that someone should invent *writers'* tool belts, because writers need a lot of tools, too. You already learned about tools like magic pencils and vowel charts, and I've been glad to see you using these." I held up each tool and pretended to stick it in my writing tool belt. "Purple pens are writing tools, too," I said, and added that to my imaginary tool belt. "Today I want to add some revision tools to your tool belts.

❖ **Name the teaching point.**

Today I want to teach you that paper flaps are a kind of revision tool that can make your stories better. Writers think carefully about where to put those flaps and use them in many different places in a story to help tell a better story."

TEACHING

Tell the class about a child who reread, envisioned his content, and then revised by adding on to the end of his draft.

"I want to tell you first about a writer named George. Let me show you what George did, because you all will want to do a similar thing. First he reread his story, 'When I Saw a Falcon Eating a Pigeon.'" I held up George's book and reenacted his revision work. "He read the first page: 'Once me and my dad took a walk to the park.'" (See Figure 14–1.)

Earlier in this unit, I talked about the importance of power tools—word walls, vowel charts, alphabet chart. I'm returning to the fact that writers use tools, only now the tools make a text more malleable. In both instances, I'm capitalizing on your children's positive feelings about workers and their tools.

In this minilesson, I convey the message that revision is important by giving writers the tools of their trade. With young children, the medium is the message. If we want a child to write longer pieces, we give that child a booklet instead of a single page. If we want a child to confer with his or her partner, we create a place for doing so.

"Then he read the next page, 'And then we sat on the soccer field.' Here, George took his revision pen, like this, and added on to the end of the page." I used my revision pen and pretended to do this. "George has added the words 'to relax,' so now his book says, 'And then we sat on the soccer field *to relax.*' That part was no problem for George."

Tell the class how this same child wanted to add writing where there wasn't space. Show that the child created a flap for the added writing.

"Look what happened next. George reread the third page of his story, 'Then we saw a falcon soaring in the air.' And he got a great idea for what he could add, but when he took up his pen to add more, he realized he *had no more room!* He came to me saying, 'I can't add anything to this page. It's already full.'

"So let me show you what George did. He got a new sheet of paper and *a writing tool, these scissors,* and he did this." I modeled what George did by holding up the scissors and cutting a strip of paper.

I held up George's story. "Look!" I opened up the flap he had added and read it aloud. "'Look! It's beautiful.' My dad said, 'I agree.'

"Later in the narrative, the falcon swooped down and ate the pigeon, and George again didn't have space for the words he wanted to add ('Gulp, gulp, gulp'), and again he used scissors to cut himself an extra flap of paper to hold more of his writing. You'll be doing the same work today—and often.

Besides thinking aloud during lessons, I show the actions of revision. I want the children to picture exactly what George did and what they can do also. I explained that George scissored to create a flap so as to highlight the use of scissors—but actually in some kindergarten classrooms I find it works best to use pre-cut flaps. In this minilesson, I don't actually use the strip of paper I make; having made the strip and (I hope) my point, I now open George's draft up in such a way to show that George has affixed such a flap onto his draft.

Allow revision to feel like carpentry. Children will be drawn to revision if it is a physical and concrete process. The scissors, staples, and revision strips will help. Eventually, children will internalize this external, concrete work and use arrows and codes to accomplish the same job.

FIG. 14–1 George's story with a final phrase added on page 2

"So that is *what* George did. He used a piece of paper as an extra flap or strip to add parts of the story he forgot to tell. I was thinking that I could even cut some strips for you and put them in this basket so that you will have them nearby." I held up a basket that I had already filled with revision strips and that I had already labeled with the words *revision strips.*

ACTIVE ENGAGEMENT

Invite writers to reread and ask themselves how they might revise to make a story better.

"Will you reread our poop story with me and see if we can help one another remember yet more that we could add?"

It was morning meeting.

We were counting the days of the week with straws.

"Can you go back in your mind to that scene and picture it? Remember your readers might never have been in our classroom. They won't know what it's like in morning meeting. Can you think of anything we could add? Turn and talk."

Soon children had reconvened and were full of suggestions. I took one, and started to insert it onto the page, but then announced there was no room. Soon, based on children's prompts, I'd made a flap that I inserted into a dramatically wrong place before rereading and locating the right place.

I paused. "I think I want to write, right here, 'All of us were sitting on all parts of the rug.' But, there is no room on the page between these two sentences. No room, no problem," I said with a raise of my brows and a smile. "I have revision strips."

I took my pen and wrote my sentence on a strip. I then taped that strip in place so that I could read my story. "Did you guys see that? First you reread the story, asking yourselves how you could make the story better. Once you have something to add, and you've reread your story to figure out where to put the addition, use a flap to put writing in the spot that makes the most sense."

LINK

Send off the children with the reminder that they have several tools to make their stories better and that they are in charge of figuring out how to use them.

"Today we'll use your whole tool belt to make your writing better. Check that you're remembering your tools. Do you have a word wall?" I touched my imaginary belt and said, "Check." Then I proceded through the list of tools. "You'll start by making one story in your folder better, then you'll go to another. I can't wait to see your revision work on more of your finished stories. I bet some of you may invent whole *different* kinds of revision. Off you go."

Helping Writers Transfer Their Details from Images to Words

MADISON DREW EXTREMELY DETAILED PICTURES—so detailed that even from halfway across the room, I could tell her piece told a story with action and emotion and characters. But she had only a very short, simple sentence on each page.

I sat down next to Madison and said, "I love the way your pictures tell your story." I turned the pages and pointed to different parts of the pictures as I admired my way through her booklet. She smiled proudly and added a comment here and there. "See how we are dancing here," and "Did you notice how sad my sister is on this page?"

I paused for a moment as I turned the three-page booklet back to page 1. "Madison, you have written a story here filled with so much storytelling power. All of that power is mostly in your pictures and just a tiny bit of that power is in your words." I flipped through the pages again quickly, just gesturing at the words she had written.

"Madison," I continued, "readers need the pictures *and* the words if they are really going to understand and appreciate all the powerful parts of your storytelling." I paused because this seemed like the crucial moment in our conference. I wanted to invite Madison to show me what she could do before I made a decision about exactly what to teach her. So I said, "If I asked you to go back through this story and work hard with your words to make it better, can you show me right now what you would do?"

Madison picked up her pencil, and I turned my body toward the writer next to her to signal that I wanted this try to be Madison's independent try. My mind was still entirely on Madison, frankly, and I could sense her hesitation. I wanted to turn back, but I had deliberately decided to make sure children did the work in my conferences (not me), and supporting independence was a big part of that. So I merely said, "Go on. Reread." Then I turned back to Madison's neighbor.

I could see Madison begin to read and then write something on the first page. When she was on the third page, I turned back toward her to signal that our conference would resume.

I asked Madison if she could show me what she had added. I again turned through the pages, reading each one with her recent additions. I tried to leave space, by mostly nodding, pointing, and smiling, for her added comments, but I did not push too hard.

As I studied her revision, I made a decision about what to teach Madison in this conference. I needed to teach her not a strategy, but a stance.

"Madison," I said. "I can tell from looking at your illustrations that you are the sort of person who doesn't just throw something on the page, then wipe your hands off and say, 'I'm done.' When you draw, you make a picture, then pull back and look it over, then think of more to add. You keep at it until it's work you are proud of. Today, you showed me you can do that same sort of keep-at-it work with your writing. From this forward, never ever do less than your best as a writer."

MID-WORKSHOP TEACHING
Remind Writers to Make Their Stories Easier to Read

"Guys, look up again. All eyes up here and pencils down, please. I was just sitting at a table of writers and so many of them were remembering to make writing easy for other people to read. Shavon saw our chart. Then he started to reread his story looking for ways to make it easier to read. He realized that he did not really need to use a flap to fix smaller things like adding more letters for more sounds in a word or making capital letters where he needed them."

I held up his writing. "See here, and here, too? Shavon just crossed out and fixed things. Will all of you remember to make your writing easy to read?"

Using Revision Tools

Draw students' attention to a student innovation on revision—in this case, using a flap to add dialogue.

As the writers returned to the rug, fresh from their attempts to use flaps and purple pens to make their writing better, I began. "Guys, I wanted to share with you what Liam did while he was working to make his story better. Liam reread his story, and he wanted to make the people in his story talk. During the last unit, you learned how to use speech bubbles to hold what people say in a story. That's one way to add talk. But you can also add dialogue right into a story.

"Liam used flaps today to hold his dialogue. He was going to draw a speech bubble over his mom to show what she was saying, but there was no room. So, he made a speech bubble in a revision strip and taped it on the page above his mom." I showed the class the place where Liam had done this construction work.

Encourage students to innovate as they revise, as well.

I read the piece without the flap and then I read the flap. The class laughed. Ava said, "Now we know your mom is silly. What she said was so silly!"

I said, "Guys, now you have another way to make your stories better. You know that you can make people talk on revision strips."

Writing Amazing Story Beginnings

IN THIS SESSION, you'll pinpoint strategies for writing strong leads by studying mentor texts and helping students to imitate them.

GETTING READY

✔ *A Chair for My Mother,* by Vera B. Williams, *Owl Moon,* by Jane Yolen, or other familiar books with great leads (see Teaching)

✔ Sample piece of writing (a child's or your own) where the lead has been revised (see Active Engagement)

✔ Sample student work to model thoughtful beginnings to each page of a story (see Share)

D URING THE FIRST TWO SESSIONS IN THIS BEND, you have been encouraging your writers to mostly go back to finished pieces and try making them better. You will do that again during this session, but because this day is about making strong beginnings, you might also ask your writers to start a new story. Your writers might begin something new with a new kind of beginning.

When it comes right down to it, how you begin matters more than almost anything else. Beginnings set the stage and set up expectations. And, for kindergarten writers, in a story with very few total lines of writing, a more skilled beginning can improve their stories tremendously.

A review of your children's writing will no doubt suggest that many of them could profit from some attention to leads. Quite a few of their leads probably sound like captions for illustrations rather than story openings. Many children probably begin their stories like this: "This is me at the park." "Here I am." Other children will summarize rather than retell events. For example, one child began, "I go to the park a lot and sometimes I . . ." This minilesson, then, is designed to give children strategies for revising their leads. The work here both aligns with the Common Core State Writing Standards but also extends into analytical craft work (RL.K.1) because writers think about the purposes behind writerly moves.

The challenge in planning a minilesson like this is that you need to understand what your children are currently doing (and trying to do) when they write leads, so that you can put your finger on something you could teach that would really help. There are a zillion things you could say about effective leads, and you need to choose among them.

You might think about your own writing process and try to articulate how you go about generating leads. Contrast your process with the processes you believe your children are using. You'll probably come to the conclusion that for starts, chances are good that most of your kindergarten writers are not *choosing* a way to begin their stories. They are just starting by writing the first thing that comes to mind.

COMMON CORE STATE STANDARDS: W.K.3, RFS.K.2, SL.K.1, L.K.1, L.K.2.a,c,d

Looking at leads in books your children already know and love and trying to name why these leads are lovable can be a way to give your kids a sense that leads matter, and a knowledge of some possible ways to begin a story. Your hope is that children will begin to have their antennae out to notice what other writers—both published and in the class—have done, thinking, "I could try that too."

"Beginnings matter more than almost anything else because they set the stage and set up expectations."

This minilesson was designed to challenge children to try to mimic mentor leads. The hope is that it will raise children's awareness and give them knowledge of what makes for effective leads. In the end, the minilesson can make it more likely that children include rewriting one's lead as part of their revision process.

Writing Amazing Story Beginnings

CONNECTION

Tell children that a strong beginning draws the reader in, making them want to hear more, and that they can study the beginnings of authors they love to get ideas for strong leads.

"When I watched you revise the stories you had already written, I noticed that almost none of you thought about changing your beginning, your lead.

"What you need to know is that famous authors think that the start to a story is one of the most important parts of the story and may work for hours on that part alone. They want to write a beginning that is like the warm smile of a friend and the tug of her hand as she gets you to sit down and listen."

❖ **Name the teaching point.**

"Today I want to teach you that one of the best ways to become a better writer is to look closely at the work of authors we love and to think, 'What did this writer do that I could try?' Because the lead to a story is really important, authors study other writers' leads and learn ways to revise their own."

TEACHING

Tell the children that just as they often learn from experts in sports, today they'll study an expert writer.

"Have you ever wanted to learn to do something in sports—like throw a Frisbee or do a yoyo trick—and then *watched the experts* to figure out what *they're* doing? You probably watched the expert do the same thing again and again, really trying to get the feel for how to do the thing she is so good at. Let's do that now. Because we want to learn how to write great beginnings, let's look closely and admire what some of the authors we know do to start a great story."

Rereading is an incredibly valuable activity, especially for writers who want to study how an author has constructed a text. We read to understand what a text says, and then return to the text again, thinking about the techniques the author has used. When we reread a text, we can notice technique. This close analytic reading work is very much in line with the priorities of the Common Core.

As children grow older, it will not only be important for them to emulate mentor texts, but also to articulate what the author has done.

Ask the children to join you in thinking about what the author has done as you read and then reread the beginning from a familiar book.

"Let's look at *A Chair for My Mother*, by Vera B. Williams, because we've been reading that book. You remember the main thing at the start of the book is that the little girl collects coins in the big green jar. Listen to Vera's lead. Will you think, 'How is she starting her story?'" I read slowly with pauses and eye contact to help the children notice Vera's way of starting the story.

> *My mother works as a waitress in the Blue Tile Diner. After school I meet her there. Then her boss, Josephine, gives me a job too. I wash the salts and peppers and fill the ketchups. One time I peeled all the onions for onion soup. When I finish, Josephine says, "Good work, honey" and pays me. And every time, I put half of my money into the jar.*

"Did you see how I read the beginning slowly, really trying to enjoy and appreciate it? That is the kind of reading you need to do if you are going to learn how to be a better writer by studying published writers. I'm going to read this beginning again, and let's all think really hard about what Vera does to start her story so maybe we'll get ideas for how we can start our stories." I reread the beginning. "Would you turn and talk with your partner about what Vera B. Williams does that we could do in our stories?"

I listened as children talked. Aiden told his partner, "She tells about the salt."

I nodded and added, "So do you think good beginnings tell about the salt? Should you tell about the salt in your story?" Aiden laughed and then said, "NO!" He added, "She washes the salt and pepper things."

I nodded and did the work of generalizing for him. "You are right. She starts the story by telling about small, precise actions that she does."

Reiterate and clarify what the author has done that you hope children emulate when they write their beginnings.

"Writers, I think more of you are onto something. Vera Williams didn't just say, 'Here I am at my mother's job.' She told us the exact details about what she is doing. Right in the first lines, she says, 'I wash the salts and peppers and fill the ketchups.'"

Choose a book your children know well that does start with action or dialogue, avoiding those with a long wind-up narrative.

One of the best things about teaching young children is that they say the darndest things. Aiden's comment made me want to laugh, but of course I maintained a straight face.

ACTIVE ENGAGEMENT

Ask the class to help one student revise his beginning.

"Writers, we saw that instead of saying, 'Here I am at my mother's job.' Vera has told about how she washed the salt and pepper shakers at the diner where her mother works. Writers often begin with tiny details.

"Would you and your partner listen while I reread the beginning of one of Eric's stories, and see if you can come up with a suggestion for Eric? Eric started his story about our Halloween parade by saying, 'This is me when I had a parade in school.' You remember our Halloween parade. If Eric was going to revise his beginning and start by telling a tiny detail, what could he say? Tell your partner."

I gave the students a moment to discuss, and then prompted, "Do you remember the thunderstorm during our parade? The weather is a detail that really helps at the start of the story."

After giving them another moment, I said, "Guys, would you look up please. I heard Kevin and Ava say that they would begin by writing, 'The clouds were dark and spooky.' Jack said he would start with, 'It was dark like night.'" I paused so that we could feel the power of these much stronger beginnings. It really is amazing. Changing the beginning can change the whole way a story grabs you.

LINK

Remind the students of the new ways they've just learned to grab readers' attention with a strong beginning.

"Today, I know you will draw on your entire toolkit to make your stories as good as they can be—or to write a new story that will be the best in the world. As you revise your stories, keep in mind that beginnings are especially important. So if you are fixing a lead or thinking about making one for a new story, you might think about writing with tiny details like Vera. Or you may begin with weather like Eric did in his story.

"And, now that you know this big writing secret about how writers always pay attention to beginnings, you will probably start to listen to the reading of stories differently. You won't be able to help yourself. You can admire what writers of other books do to begin their stories, and you can then try to mimic their best moves. Off you go now to tell true stories that make us listen right from the very first page."

When I was unsure how to start an earlier book about teaching writing, I went to Pulitzer Prize–winning writer Don Murray for help. He said, "It's the same as when you first greet someone on the street. If you don't know what else to say, talk about the weather." I began that book with "The sunlight streamed in through the windows of Room 304 as I pulled my chair alongside . . ." I told this to a group of K–2 teachers and soon literally thousands of young kids were starting their stories with the weather and finding this added a very literary feel. A story that had begun, "I went to the park," now started, "One rainy gray morning, I went to the park."

Teaching Kids What Their Jobs Are in Writing Conferences

AS YOUR YEAR UNFOLDS, you'll sometimes want to use the work time during a workshop to help coach your students into the expectations you have for them in general—not tied to any special unit. For example, you'll no doubt have found that conferences with kids can be hard because they don't yet grasp their roles in them. So you might explicitly teach children the jobs you hope they do in conferences. I recently gathered four youngsters together to start this teaching.

"I pulled the four of you together because I wanted to teach you all the same thing at the same time. Ever since the start of the year, during each day's writing workshop, you've seen me come around and confer with you about your writing. When I confer with you, I have a job that I'm doing. But *you* also have a job in these conferences, and I'm not sure you know your job. Today I want to teach you what your job is in a writing conference.

"I don't know if you realize it or not, but every time I confer, I always start by doing the same things. First, I watch. You'll see me draw a chair near to you. Usually I don't say anything for a few minutes. I'm watching what you do as a writer—and your job during this first part of a conference is to keep doing what you do as a writer. Don't stop because I'm close. Don't say, 'May I read my piece to you?' Keep working so I can watch what you do when you write.

"Then next, I usually ask a question. I might ask, 'What are you doing as a writer?' or 'What are you working on?'

"This is the time when you have a big job. Let me show you what you sometimes do—and what I wish you'd do. You all be researchers and notice the difference. Omid has said he'll be the teacher; I'll be the writer."

I stage-whispered to Omid, "Omid, say, 'Hi, what are you working on?'" He did, and I replied abruptly, turning my response into a caricature, "My teddy bear's birthday party."

MID-WORKSHOP TEACHING
Revising Action Words to Sharpen Small Details

"Writers, I need to interrupt you all for just a minute. Ava just made me realize that when writing details, it is especially wise to write more detailed action words. Ava's story had started like this, 'I was walking to the park with my dad.' She realized she could make actions more detailed if she asked herself, 'How?' So she asked, 'How was I walking?'

"Now Ava's beginning goes: 'I was skipping to the park with my dad.'

"Some of the rest of you may want to find your action words and make them more detailed by asking, 'How?' Try it right now."

As Students Continue Working . . .

"Would you look up from your writing for a second, please? I just wanted to remind you all that when you are revising your beginnings, you can use flaps if there is no room on your page," and I held one up. "You can put a flap right over the first beginning and then try to do a better beginning on it."

Then I said to the kids, "You often do this. You just tell the *topic* of your writing. Here's the sort of answer I *wish* you'd give." I stage-whispered again to Omid, "Omid, ask me again."

Omid again asked, "Hi, what are you working on?"

Again I role-played being a child. "I'm writing about my teddy bear birthday." (Here, in an aside, I name what I just did: "I told the topic I'm writing about.") "*And* I am trying to write important details about the teddy bear birthday—not boring details, but *important* details." (In another aside I say, "That's the work I am doing as a writer.") "I am crossing out the boring parts.

"So, writers, could you tell the person next to you why it's better to say my topic *and* to say 'I am trying to write the important details about the teddy bear birthday—not just the boring details'?" I listened in as the partners talked to each other.

"I'm hearing you say that at the start of a conference, when I ask, 'What are you working on?' your job is not only to say the topic—the teddy bear birthday—but also to say *what you are trying to do as a writer*.

"So right now, in your mind, could each of you get ready for a writing conference? I want you all to pretend that it is writing time. Pull out your folders. I am going to come to each of you and ask, 'What are you working on as a writer?' If I am not talking to you, keep writing, but as you are working, you might want to be thinking about how you will answer me in your conference."

Each child began writing, and I moved from one to the other asking about their work. After I had asked each child, I said, "So guys, remember that our charts can help you talk about your writing work. Any time we work together, anything I teach and you try, can become what you talk about when you describe your writing work to me.

"There is one other giant job that you have in a writing conference, or in a small group or minilesson, for that matter. Every time someone is teaching you something, you need to try to learn what you are taught, remember it, and use it. So, we just worked on something in this group. Would you turn to the person next to you and tell them what you learned in this group?"

I listened in to each partnership and then I called them back together. "So that's it, guys," I said. "Today you learned that in every conference you have two big jobs. You need to talk about your writing work and you need to try to learn, remember, and use what you have been taught. I can't wait until our next conference. Off you go. Back to your work."

Transition Words Help to Begin a New Page

Using a child's work as an example, encourage students to write thoughtful beginnings to each page of a story.

"Writers, eyes, please. I just want to share with you what Patrick and I were talking about." I waited a few seconds longer because my teaching was worth their attention for sure. I began, "When I sat down next to Patrick, he had already revised the beginning of his story. He was turning to page two and he read it to me. After he had listened to himself read the next page out loud, he said the most amazing thing!

"Do you want to know what he said? He said, 'The beginning of this page is not very good.' He asked me if there could be a new beginning on the second page, too. Patrick's question is so smart. Writers, the truth is that the beginning of the story matters a lot, but so does the beginning of each page. Every time someone turns the page in your booklet, they need to understand how the new page goes with the pages that came before it."

Encourage your students to try out using transition words as they move from one part of a story to the next.

"There are words that help a reader understand how the pages and parts of the story fit together. Published writers call these words 'transition words.' Transition is a fancy way to say move from one thing to another. Transition words are words that help the reader move from one part or one page to another.

"Often those words sound like they talk about time. Words like *later*, *after that*, *suddenly*, or *it was a long time* can all be used to begin new pages so that the reader understands how the new page is connected to the pages that came before. So now we are thinking about how every page needs a beginning that helps the reader understand the story better."

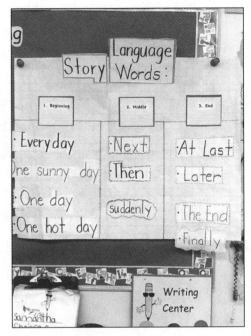

FIG. 15–1   Storytelling transitions

Writers Work with Partners to Answer Readers' Questions

IN THIS SESSION, you'll teach students how to revise their own work and help each other by offering strategies for peer partnerships.

GETTING READY

✔ Narrative Writing Checklist, Grades K and 1 (see Active Engagement) ✪

✔ Two "Conferring Center" signs posted in the room (see Link)

✔ Children's current writing brought to the minilesson

✔ Post-it notes to mark reactions to student work (see Share)

TODAY'S MINILESSON IS A CLASSIC. IT'S BEEN a staple in writing workshop instruction since the days when it was a brand-new and still preposterous idea to imagine young children authoring their own books, and even more outlandish to suggest five- and six-year-olds could revise their writing. Even then, one of the biggest challenges in workshop teaching was the teacher–student ratio. If five- and six-year-olds were going to be lured to revise, it depended on the strong supportive presence of a teacher. This meant that writing workshop teachers soon found themselves rushing from one child to the next to the next, cajoling each to add on, to clarify.

It was inevitable, then, that a minilesson would be developed that said to children, "You've got to learn to be your own writing teacher," and it was inevitable that such a minilesson would become a mainstay of any workshop.

If you are going to pass the baton to children, inviting them to reread their own writing, to anticipate the questions readers will ask, and to decide on their own ways to revise their writing, you need to be ready to welcome their efforts. They won't revise as you would! One child announced that she wanted to make a better ending to her story. So she erased the straightforward words, *The End*, and made an elaborate, striped and polka-dotted version of the same two words! Another child told me he wanted to add excitement in his story. I came back ten minutes later to find that he'd added exclamation marks—whole lines of them—throughout his piece. Be ready to enjoy your children's efforts.

COMMON CORE STATE STANDARDS: W.K.3, W.K.5, W.1.3, RL.K.1, RL.K.2, RL.K.3, SL.K.1, SL.K.2, SL.K.3, L.K.1, L.K.2

Writers Work with Partners to Answer Readers' Questions

CONNECTION

Tell the class that at one point during the last session, you found a long line of kids behind you needing help. Tell them that you'll teach each of them to be a writing teacher.

"Writers, yesterday when I was working with Luke, I looked up and saw a line of kids waiting for my help. And I have been thinking about that line ever since. Because you are all working so hard to revise your writing, you've been needing more of my help, so the line has gotten longer. But when you are waiting for my help, you lose writing time."

❧ **Name the teaching point.**

"Driving to school today, I realized what I need to teach you. I want to teach you that there's not one writing teacher in this room—there are twenty-eight of you. To be a writing teacher, you need to *really listen* to the writer's draft, trying to really understand it, and you need to notice the places where you go, 'Huh?' to help the writer make those parts clear."

TEACHING

Demonstrate how children can be writing teachers for one another. First, teach them to read the other's writing.

"So let's say I am six years old and I come to you with my writing and I say, 'Help me, help me. I'm done. Help me, help me.' Do you think you start telling me (and I asked in a bossy, pedant way, pointing and giving orders), 'Do this. Do that. Do this.'?" The children joined me in shaking their heads and exclaiming, "No!"

"You are right. Instead, to be a good writing teacher, you say, 'Can I hear your writing?'"

"If I read my writing to you, do you think you listen like this?" and I picked my teeth, leaned back in my chair, acting utterly distracted.

Everyone chimed, "No!"

◆ COACHING

You get right to the point. "There's a problem in this class," you say. Children will be anticipating the solution.

I like to play up the "Help me, help me" plea, dramatizing a needy writer. I also dramatize the bossy partner. All of this is meant as a drumroll to the point of a minilesson.

"So I'll read my story, and will you be great writing teachers, trying to really listen, to really understand? If there are parts you really love, that you can picture well, be sure to tell me. If there are confusing parts, let me know that too. Get me to explain those parts and to fix up the confusing parts. You ready?"

Then I opened my story, written on chart paper, and put it on the easel.

> On Saturday I went apple picking. We had cider and donuts. Then we got two baskets for apples. We went to pick them. Then we spilled them. Then we went to pick some more. Then we came home.

Demonstrate how to pay attention to your reactions as a reader of your partner's writing.

"How about I read my piece again, and when you feel like saying, 'Wow,' to something in my story, put your thumb up? And, if you hear something in my story that makes you say, 'Huh,' will you make a little 'Huh?' gesture?" and I demonstrated with a shrug.

I read a little bit of my story, and Lilly put her finger up right away. "I like something. I want to wow that part where you said, 'We had cider and donuts.' That part sounds good."

"So you like the details I put in there, about the cider and the donut? I'm going to add *jelly* donut," I said, and I did. Then I continued reading, saying, "I hope you hear another great detail and give me more wows." I read a little bit more of my story. Kevin and Aiden were suddenly whispering to each other. I paused in my reading, and they did not even seem to notice. They were still whispering. "What's up, guys?" I called. Startled, Kevin said, "You went to pick them, and then you spilled them. That is confusing."

"Yeah," Aiden added. "How did you get 'em? The apples."

"Good. I love how you were paying attention to my reading, and then it was almost as if you could *not* pay attention anymore because you were so confused. That is how it feels when something does not make sense. It is important for the writer to know those *Huh?* parts."

Turning back to my story, I said, "Maybe I could tell you something about how we got to use a ladder to reach the high branches for the reddest apples. I could write that part here," and I pointed to the spot on my paper, "in between getting the baskets and spilling the apples."

As you read this story, don't use your intonation to make it clearer than it is. The story is meant to be confusing! Read it so that the children think, "Huh?"

ACTIVE ENGAGEMENT

"Now it is your turn. I want you guys to be writing partners for each other. Partner 1, would you choose and read one of your finished stories to your partner? Partner 2, I need you guys to listen and pay attention to your reactions, noticing times when you feel like saying, 'Wow,' or 'Huh?' Partner 1, hold up your story when you are ready." I waited a few seconds until a blue sea of writing folders were waving before me, and then I said, "Go."

As I listened in on the partners working together, I saw many of the listening partners only listening. They did not seem to be paying attention to their reactions and, therefore, seemed to be doing little to help improve the quality of their partner's story. I interrupted.

Remind children about the Narrative Writing Checklist to help them remember what to pay attention to and what to notice in their partners' stories.

"Guys, would you just turn your heads this way?" I waited a beat." Guys, I noticed that many of the Partner 2s were *only* listening. It was as if you did not know what to say to your partner if you want to 'wow' the writing. Remember, you know a lot now about what makes a strong story!"

I pointed to a few bullets on our Narrative Writing Checklist. "These are some of the things you can be listening for when your partner reads their story to you. This checklist can help you talk back to your partner." I quickly read the first few points on the kindergarten list:

- I told, drew, and wrote a whole story.
- I had a page that showed what happened first.
- My story indicated who was there, what they did, and how the characters felt.

Joining my hands together, I said, "Now, try again."

This time when I listened in on the partners, I started to hear some feedback. Slowly, the listening partners began to offer up their ideas. For instance, Camila told her partner, "I love all of the different faces on your people."

Then Camila said the most amazing thing and offered me the most brilliant teaching tip. Camila said, "Maybe I can try to make my people more like the ones you make." It was almost like a slow-motion moment. I listened in on a few more partnerships, and then convened the group.

"You were much better this time. I knew there were so many strong writing teachers in this room. I saw so many of you using our Narrative Writing Checklist to remind you what makes a good story. I know our partnerships will help us make writing that wows the world."

The reason that we say, "Read Partner 1's writing . . ." is that children waste a lot of time deciding who will do what. We don't have time to spare in a minilesson. The reason children only read the first page of one child's writing is that we carefully curtail minilessons so they don't last longer than ten minutes.

After a deep breath, a smile, and some generous eye contact, I said, "Before you all go off to write, I want to tell you what Camila said. She was wowed by something her partner did in her writing, and then she said, 'Maybe I could try that same thing in my own writing.'"

I partially closed my eyes and gasped a little, trying to signal to my kindergartners that this was something that was *something*. "What Camila realized is that being a writing partner is not just about helping someone else make their story stronger. Being a writing partner can also help you learn to make your own writing stronger. Anything that wows you about your partner's writing can be something you try to do in your own writing, too. That is so cool!"

LINK

Remind children to go to one another at the Conferring Centers today, and from now on.

"So, guys, now you know that there are so many other writing teachers in this class. You also know one way you might help each other make better stories. You can go to your writing partner whenever you feel like you really need someone to listen carefully and react to your writing. Writing can feel lonely as you work to put your own ideas on your own paper all by yourself. Today you learned a way to work together as partners so that writing never has to be lonely again.

"Off you go," I said as I nudged them all away from me, and to their work.

Narrative Writing Checklist

	Kindergarten	NOT YET	STARTING TO	YES!	Grade 1	NOT YET	STARTING TO	YES!
	Structure				**Structure**			
Overall	I told, drew, and wrote a whole story.	☐	☐	☐	I wrote about when I did something.	☐	☐	☐
Lead	I had a page that showed what happened first.	☐	☐	☐	I tried to make a beginning for my story.	☐	☐	☐
Transitions	I put my pages in order.	☐	☐	☐	I put my pages in order. I used words such as *and* and *then, so*.	☐	☐	☐
Ending	I had a page that showed what happened last in my story.	☐	☐	☐	I found a way to end my story.	☐	☐	☐
Organization	My story had a page for the beginning, a page for the middle, and a page for the end.	☐	☐	☐	I wrote my story across three or more pages.	☐	☐	☐
	Development				**Development**			
Elaboration	My story indicated who was there, what they did, and how the characters felt.	☐	☐	☐	I put the picture from my mind onto the page. I had details in pictures and words.	☐	☐	☐
Craft	I drew and wrote some details about what happened.	☐	☐	☐	I used labels and words to give details.	☐	☐	☐
	Language Conventions				**Language Conventions**			
Spelling	I could read my writing.	☐	☐	☐	I used all I knew about words and chunks of words (*at, op, it*, etc.) to help me spell.	☐	☐	☐
	I wrote a letter for the sounds I heard.	☐	☐	☐	I spelled all the word wall words right and used the word wall to help me spell other words.	☐	☐	☐
	I used the word wall to help me spell.	☐	☐	☐		☐	☐	☐

Assessment-Based Small Groups

AS YOUR UNIT APPROACHES THE FINAL STRETCH, you'll want to do some assessment. One of the most powerful ways to do this is to ask children to leave the day's writing at their workspaces when they head off to a special—to gym or music. This means you'll have forty minutes to do a quick assessment.

Decide on one lens that you'll use for assessing their work. Say, for example, you decide to look at their work with the question "Is it readable?" in mind, with the follow-up question, "If not, why not?"

Or, alternatively, you could examine their writing by asking, "Have they been revising?" We looked with this latter lens, asking if there was *substantial* revision, *some* revision, or *no* revision.

If we'd found that the work from half the class was in the No Revision pile, we would have rethought the trajectory of the unit, deciding to spend a few more days supporting revision. In fact, however, far more children were in the Some Revision pile.

We decided the writers whose work was in the No Revision pile could benefit from a guided practice small group where we walked children through actually revising one of their own stories. As we led this group, we watched the students to try to figure out what had made each resistant to revision so that we could try to make the strategy more attractive for them.

The writers whose folders were in the Some Revision pile needed us to help them make this part of the writing process more consistent for them. We formed a small group and challenged them to do what they had done on one piece on as many pieces as possible. We wanted these beginning writers to repeat the behavior again and again, until they could not even imagine writing without revising.

The writers whose work was in the A Lot of Revision pile needed closer study. These kids needed teaching that named the specific ways in which they were using revision, and they needed feedback on whether their revisions were making their writing better or worse.

MID-WORKSHOP TEACHING   Honoring Stories by Encouraging Writers to Practice Reading Aloud

"Writers, eyes up, please. You've been writing for twenty minutes, so I thought you might want to get help from your partner.

"Guys, I want you to remember that in order for your partner to help, you need to read your piece well like it is read-aloud time and you are the teacher, reading aloud *your* book."

I stood next to Maya and reached down for her ladybug story. I said, "Listen to me read Maya's story." Then I read.

I saw a ladybug.

The ladybug climbed on my arm.

I counted the spots.

"Did you guys hear the way I read Maya's story like it is a treasure? You'll want to read your story like that as well. Before you go to work with your partner, rehearse by reading your story to yourself. Point under each word as you practice. Really hear your story. Would you try that now?"

After a minute, I channeled the children to work in their partnerships.

As Students Continue Working . . .

Later, after writers had resumed writing, I called, "Writers, don't forget to think about your partner as you are writing. Remember that your writing partner is really your first reader. As you write and reread, be sure to keep asking yourself, 'Did I do enough to make this clear? Will this *wow* my partner?'"

Critical Rereading

Give partners one more strategy for their work—Post-it notes with exclamation points or question marks can show writers where their story is strong or where there are questions.

"Guys, Liam said that sometimes when he reads the books in his book baggie during reading time, he feels *wow* or *huh*. He's been putting exclamation marks with 'Wow' parts and question marks on the 'Huh?' parts. So I started to think maybe you could be readers of your *own* writing, and you can put 'Wow' and 'Huh?' marks on Post-its in your own books, and then use those marks to nudge you to make your writing even better. Are you game for trying that?" The writers began rereading.

Fun With My Play Date!

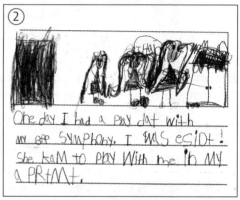

One day I had a play date with my BFF Symphony. I was excited! She came to play with me in my apartment.

Then my BFF went in my room. When my BFF was in my room she wanted to play with my toys.

FIG. 16–1   Juliette's play date story

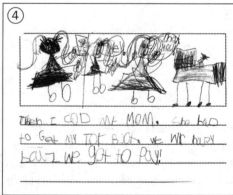

Then I called my mom. She had to get my toy box. We were happy because we got to play!

Writers Use All They Know to Select and Revise a Piece to Publish

IN THIS SESSION, you'll help writers choose a piece for their celebration. You'll model strategies for making a story more meaningful and help students begin their revision on their own pieces.

GETTING READY

✔ Supplies for your writing center, including a "toolbox" of scissors, revision strips, markers, and tape

✔ Narrative Writing Checklist, Grades K and 1 (Conferring and Small-Group Work) ✎

✔ "What Makes Writing Easy to Read" chart, posted

✔ Your own narrative story, perhaps from a time when you were young, in draft form (see Teaching)

✔ An easel

✔ Writing folders (see Active Engagement)

✔ Shared writing from Sessions 13 and 14 (see Share)

MANY WRITERS HAVE WRITTEN about the power of a deadline, claiming that the more accurate term would be *lifeline*. Writers will say, "Knowing that I have just a few more days before the draft is pulled from my hands, before it is sent to the presses, spurs me into action." The same can happen for children.

Of course, early in their kindergarten year, youngsters don't yet grasp what publication really involves. It's your job, then, to help children understand that writers choose their best work, and then fix it up and fancy it up before it is made into an official book and released to the public.

As you induct children into this process, be sure to value all the steps leading up to publication. For example, you could skirt right over the fact that writers first choose their best work . . . or you could turn even that portion of the process into an educative one. After all, determining which story is one's best can be complicated, demanding, delightful work!

So our suggestion is to imbue the process of preparation for publication with grandeur and significance. Make it matter.

COMMON CORE STATE STANDARDS: W.K.3, W.K.5, W.K.6, RFS.K.1, RFS.K.2, RFS.K.3, RL.K.3, SL.K.1, SL.K.2, SL.K.3, L.K.1, L.K.2

Writers Use All They Know to Select and Revise a Piece to Publish

CONNECTION

Celebrate the work students have been doing and set them up to make one story out of all the stories they have written the best it can be.

"Guys, today is a big day. You have worked for several weeks learning so many strategies to help you make amazing, 'Easy to Read' stories. Your folders are stuffed, bursting with all of the stories you have told. Now, with just a few days left before you pause your writing work to celebrate what you all have learned, it is time to really focus. It is time to break out all of your tools. Magic pencils and personal word walls. Flaps and vowel charts. Every tool you have, you need to have out and ready to help do the big work of getting just one story ready to be presented!"

I moved over in front of the writing center. "In order to get ready for today and for the next few days, I have made sure that the writing center is reloaded with supplies and tools, and it is also reorganized to make sure that every tool you need is ready and at your fingertips. You can also see that our writing charts are all here, too, above the writing center. When you are writing at your seats or with your partners, you will know exactly where to look when you need advice on how else you might make your stories better."

✿ **Name the teaching point.**

"Today I want to teach you that writers get ready to publish by choosing the story they want to share with the world. Then, they use all they know to make their stories come to life and be easy to read."

TEACHING

Model the revision process for writers by reading aloud your own story.

"Guys, let me show you a way to get started preparing a piece of writing for a celebration. I have a story here that I love about a play date I had with my best friend when I was your age." I held up my three-page story. "If I want to make this piece of writing extra special, I first need to reread it and remember the time that I wrote about. I think, 'Have I told you about why this time was special to me?'" I hung each of the pages of my story up on the easel and I read.

◆ COACHING

I know this unit is coming to a close and so it makes sense to harken back to the beginning of the unit, reflecting on the journey.

I try to help children understand that revision is a way to honor and care for one's writing. Too often, youngsters grow up thinking of revision as a form of punishment.

Lee and I played catch in her yard. We were sweaty. It was fun.

Lee said, "Let's each lunch." I ran to get my bag from out of the sun.

We both smelled something stinky. It was my lunch. I was embarrassed.

"I think I can add more. I didn't put down that this was my first play date ever. I should put that in. And I didn't tell that when my lunch was stinky, Lee didn't laugh at me." I quickly wrote those two sentences into my story. "Did you see how I first reread and remembered, and then I added what was missing to make sure I told why the time was special to me?"

ACTIVE ENGAGEMENT

Set writers up to reread their own writing.

"So today, writers, you are going to start getting one of your stories ready for publication. And I'm hoping you'll be able to do that work without all lining up beside me saying, 'Help me! Help me!'

"Right now, will you think, 'What is the first thing I need to do to get ready to publish?'" I gave the children a moment to think. Then I said, "Thumbs up if you thought that first you are going to look over all your stories and choose the one you like best to publish." Many children so signaled.

"Will you read through your pieces like this?" I asked, and tore through a stack in a halfhearted fashion. "No!" "Will you read them like this?" and I studiously looked between two stories, setting one aside. "Yes!" "After you choose a story to publish, you'll reread it to remember that time. And you'll also think about—what, writers? Turn and talk. What will you think about when you reread the story you want to publish?"

Soon I heard children talk, and reconvened the group. "You are right. You'll think whether there are parts that will make readers go 'Huh?' and you'll make them more clear. And you'll ask, 'Did I tell why this time was special for me?' That can lead you to add more to your stories."

LINK

Encourage students to select their most special story from their writing folders.

"I want you guys to try this, getting started right here on the rug. Start reading through your folders to find the story that is most important to you. Do that now." I moved around the rug, asking no one in particular and everyone in general, "Is that your most special one? Can you imagine making that one super special?" Once I saw children reading carefully, I dispersed them.

FIG. 17–1   My "Lee" story

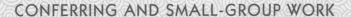

Organizing Work and Using the Checklists to Help Students Revise

SOME DAYS, your job during independent work time can have phases. You can plan what you'll do in the first half of work time and in the second half of work time.

Today, you'll want to be sure that writers have committed to a story. Perhaps you'll ask kids to place a small pink Post-it on this story, and have them store it in the front of the green side of their folder.

After that, you'll want to reach as many kids as possible to help them reread the story, lay the checklist next to the piece, and then consider ways to revise the story by using the checklist as a guide. To help children know what it means to do the work on the checklist, you'll want to have your draft on hand.

(continues)

MID-WORKSHOP TEACHING   **Offering a Visual Strategy for Revision**

"Would you all look up and pause your work for a moment? I wanted to show you what Jane and I were working on during our conference. Jane took the staple out of her three-page booklet," I pretended to remove a staple, "so that she could spread her story across the table." I spread Jane's three pages across the desk as I said this. "When she could see all the pages of her story at the same time, she could really think about how she might make those pages tell her story in even better ways. She could really see what was missing. She could really see the holes in her work."

Looking around the room, I said, "You may want to do the same kind of taking your book apart in order to add stuff that will make your story better when you put it back together again." Children began to take apart their books. I coached, "Make sure you lay your story out in order from left to right, this way, so that it makes sense when you read it."

Aiden said, "My picture on this page is *waaaaay* better than the pictures on this page and this page."

Zoe said, "You gotta take more time on the other pages."

I walked around the room and called, "Everyone read your story now. Notice how the pages go together and how they look side by side. Do all three pages go together in a way that makes sense? Do some pages look like you worked on them harder?" I leaned over and touched Camila's paper and said, "Are there some lines not filled with words? Does every page have purple pen or flaps or speech bubbles?"

"Fix your story right now—don't wait—if you just saw something that needs work. This spread-it-out strategy along with the read-it-out-loud strategy are two ways to figure out what needs more work."

As Students Continue Working . . .

"If you don't have at least one tool with you right now, you are probably having some trouble doing the work of making writing that shows off the humongous amount you did during this unit. Everyone, right now, take a second and hold up

your tool." All kinds of hands, all differently equipped, shot into the air. "Take a look around. Notice all of the different tools. Keep some of them in mind for your work over the next few days."

When I sat down next to Jane, she was working on her pink Post-it note piece. I pulled her checklist out. I took the staple out of her story so that we could spread the pages out in front of her from left to right. I said, "Jane, sometimes when you are getting ready to celebrate, it helps to spread out your work so you can see all of it at the same time, without needing to turn the pages. Let's put your checklist up above the pages of your book so that you can keep looking at it to remind yourself of all the things you could be doing to make this story better."

Jane said, "I am making sure this story is easy to read. I gotta get more vowels, I know, and sometimes I can't write all the words from the wall right." I said, "So, you are looking for words that need more vowels, and you are looking for words that are on our wall to check them for correct spelling." She nodded. "For the vowel work, you can use our vowel chart to help you." I pulled it out. "For the word wall work, you need to remind yourself of all of the words that are there by reading the whole wall before you search for those words and then check them in your story."

"Okay," Jane said.

"Before I leave," I interrupted one last time, "what will you do after vowel and word wall words?"

"I think I need to add more," she said. Then, "I really want some of those flap thingies on my story for the celebration. I like those!"

This kind of conference can be repeated for the rest of the day and for the rest of the week. When kids don't know what to do, I refer them to our mentor pieces. When kids know what to do, I ask them to teach others what they've done.

Narrative Writing Checklist

	Kindergarten	NOT YET	STARTING TO	YES!	Grade 1	NOT YET	STARTING TO	YES!
	Structure				**Structure**			
Overall	I told, drew, and wrote a whole story.	☐	☐	☐	I wrote about when I did something.	☐	☐	☐
Lead	I had a page that showed what happened first.	☐	☐	☐	I tried to make a beginning for my story.	☐	☐	☐
Transitions	I put my pages in order.	☐	☐	☐	I put my pages in order. I used words such as *and* and *then, so.*	☐	☐	☐
Ending	I had a page that showed what happened last in my story.	☐	☐	☐	I found a way to end my story.	☐	☐	☐
Organization	My story had a page for the beginning, a page for the middle, and a page for the end.	☐	☐	☐	I wrote my story across three or more pages.	☐	☐	☐
	Development				**Development**			
Elaboration	My story indicated who was there, what they did, and how the characters felt.	☐	☐	☐	I put the picture from my mind onto the page. I had details in pictures and words.	☐	☐	☐
Craft	I drew and wrote some details about what happened.	☐	☐	☐	I used labels and words to give details.	☐	☐	☐
	Language Conventions				**Language Conventions**			
Spelling	I could read my writing.	☐	☐	☐	I used all I knew about words and chunks of words (*at, op, it,* etc.) to help me spell.	☐	☐	☐
	I wrote a letter for the sounds I heard.	☐	☐	☐	I spelled all the word wall words right and used the word wall to help me spell other words.	☐	☐	☐
	I used the word wall to help me spell.	☐	☐	☐		☐	☐	☐

Writing Powerful Titles to Stories

Teach students about the power of titles. Remind them that they make readers want to read their stories.

After the children all sat on their rug spots in the meeting area, I said, "This is getting more and more exciting. I can't wait for your parents to hear your stories and to see your hard work in just a few days. Because readers are coming, I have been thinking about all of the little touches that will help your stories make more sense for them. Right now I want to talk a little bit about titles.

"Titles are a way to get readers interested in your story, to tell readers what is most important. There are many kinds of titles. I want to think about mysterious titles, which can make people want to read your story to solve the mystery."

Brainstorm an effective title for your class story.

I pulled out our "poop on the rug" story. I said, "You guys remember our 'poop on the rug' story, right? Well, if I think about a title that might help the reader know what this story is about, I could call it *Poop on the Rug*. That title totally tells what the story is about. But I am trying to also get a reader excited about reading my story, so I want to be a little mysterious. Hmmmm . . ."

I looked at the class, inviting them to talk through my silence. "Well, I could call it *The Teacher's Shoe*. That title might make people want to read the story. Readers might think, 'What kind of story would be about the teacher's shoe?'"

Suddenly Malachi shouted, "How about *What's That Smell?!*"

There was a spontaneous burst of laughter, and we all knew that Malachi's suggestion needed to be our title. I wrote that title on a blank piece of paper. Then I said, "So, now that we have found a title for our class story, I want you guys to turn and talk to your rug partner about possible titles for your celebration piece. Remember that it may take two or three tries before you find just the right title. Play around with titles, trying to give your story a name that will make readers curious to open up your book and read."

The room erupted with talk about titles. I listened in a little, and then I said, "So I have some blank paper here, and if you have an idea for your title, I want you to write it on your paper right now. If you don't have a title you love, just take the blank paper and put it in your folder. Sometimes the longer you sit with something, the easier it is to come up with a good idea."

Ending with Feelings

IN THIS SESSION, you'll help students focus on writing endings that leave readers with a strong feeling. By modeling an ending with strong emotion, you'll provide an example of the kind of ending they might try.

GETTING READY

✔ *Koala Lou*, by Mem Fox, or another book that demonstrates ending a story with a feeling (see Connection)

✔ Two pieces of writing (the children's or your own) in which the endings have been revised to show strong emotion (see Teaching and Active Engagement)

✔ A visual chart that displays the different shades of emotion (see Share)

E ARLIER IN THE YEAR, you might have noticed that many of your children ended their stories with "and then I went home" or "I went to bed." This is typical of inexperienced writers' early stories. Simply understanding that stories need to be wrapped up in some way and figuring out a way to do it is big news and cause for celebration. Endings are crucial because they are the last words a reader reads, and, therefore, they leave a lasting impression. One writer has said that poems and stories are like love affairs—you can forgive anything as long as they have a good ending. (But don't tell this to the children!)

In today's session, you encourage children to consider new ways to craft endings. In this minilesson, you teach your kindergartners that they can study ways other writers end their pieces and try out techniques they notice. Those other writers need not be famous authors—they can be other kindergartners! You'll teach children that endings often leave readers with a feeling. When youngsters add feelings to their stories, they are usually adding reactions to the events, and hand in hand with that, adding the signficance of the event. This is an important Common Core goal. This minilesson can make a big difference to your children's work.

COMMON CORE STATE STANDARDS: W.K.3, W.K.5, W.K.6, W.1.3, RFS.K.1, RFS.K.2, RFS.K.3, SL.K.1, SL.K.2, L.K.1.f, L.K.2.a,c,d

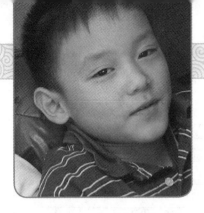

Ending with Feelings

CONNECTION

Tell the children that when they read stories they often read the endings in ways that show strong feelings. Point out that writers put those feelings there for readers to find. They can *write* strong story endings that show strong feelings.

"You've been working so hard on writing your stories, and you're getting closer to being ready to celebrate them! Did you know that in addition to *writing* strong stories, it's important to tell and read stories really well? I learned a tip about this from the author Mem Fox, who wrote *Koala Lou*—when you come to the end of a story, your voice needs to close . . . down . . . the . . . story. She says that when you read the ending of a book or a poem, your voice can make the end feel like the *amen* at the end of a prayer, or the *goodnight* at the end of a day, the dessert at the end of the meal, or the *so long* at the end of a visit.

"Listen as I read the ending of Mem's book, *Koala Lou*. You remember how Koala lost the race and crept home, sad? But then her mother found her. The book ends like this":

> Her mother said, "Koala Lou, I do love you," and she hugged her for a very long time.

"Do you hear how Mem Fox ended her story with a strong feeling—in this case, love?"

❖ **Name the teaching point.**

"Because I read endings as if they are the most special words in the world, when I write, I always go back and revise my endings to make them worthy. Today I want to teach you that one way writers write strong endings is to end their stories with a feeling. Sometimes writers just tell how they feel, but other times, writers do what Mem Fox did in *Koala Lou*. They use dialogue or actions to show a feeling."

I'm convinced that if children read their own writing aloud with reverence they'll write pieces that deserve to be read in such a manner. Teaching children to read their endings with a majestic pace will do more than almost anything to improve the qualities of those endings.

Read the final words slowly, really thinking about their meaning. "She hugged her—for a very . . . long . . . time."

TEACHING

Tell the children that writers can emulate endings in published texts.

"I love to study the work of other authors. I get ideas from what other authors do. When I find an ending I love, I look back on it and think, 'What did that author do that worked so, so well?' So watch me now as I read an ending I love, and then try to name what the author did that I could try. See if you can notice what the author does at the end.

"The story I'm going to read is written by a first-grade author named Eric (see Figure 18–1). It goes like this."

> One day me and my class went to the garden to plant bulbs.
>
> "How long do we have, Pat?" I said. I was jumping and jumping, hoping I'd have a long time, when Pat said, "Ten minutes." I was so mad. I stomped my foot. Steam was coming out of my ears. "I want more time to plant." In my head I was saying, "I need more time," it went on and on. "Pat, I need more time," I said.
>
> "Eric, you're starting to annoy me. No other kid is annoying me," [Pat said.] All the kids ran to Pat, "Pat, Eric told us we only have ten minutes." "Pat, we need more time!" "Pat," "Pat," "Pat," it went on and on and on.

"Hmmm. So what did Eric do to make a good ending? Hmmm." I reread the last few lines. As hands began to shoot up, I said, "Eric didn't just end the story with what he did: 'I went home' or 'I went to bed.' He wrote an ending that leaves readers with a strong feeling—in this case, frustration. And he did not just *say* he was frustrated, he used dialogue to show his feelings.

"So one lesson we could learn from Eric and from Mem Fox is that strong endings sometimes use a strong feeling. But the other, bigger lesson is that endings matter, and if we admire an ending that works, we can see what the author did to write that good ending."

ACTIVE ENGAGEMENT

Ask children to notice and discuss why a story's ending is so strong.

"Let's try it. I'm going to read you another story by an author named Lisa (see Figure 18–2). When I reach the end, listen to how my voice sounds, and then tell your partner what Lisa did to make such a nice ending."

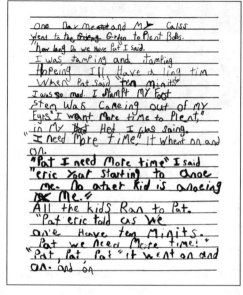

FIG. 18–1 First grader Eric has written this story.

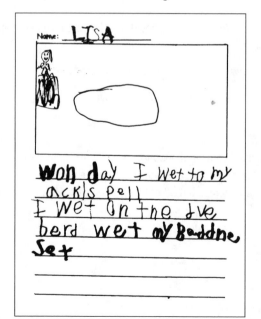

FIG. 18–2 Lisa's pool story

I read:

> One day I went to my uncle's pool.
>
> I went on the diving board with my bathing suit.
>
> I went under water. I sat under the water for three minutes. I went back up in one second. I felt like a fish.

After I read this story, the kids turned knee to knee and eye to eye to puzzle out why this was an ending to admire.

Riley told Shavon, "This ending is weird because it talks about fish."

Shavon answered, "It says how she felt, fishy. That's silly," she said and started imitating a fish.

They laughed a belly laugh together.

"Guys," I called. "So I heard you really trying to figure out what Lisa did to make such an amazing ending. It was like she read the first pages of her story, and when she got to the last page she thought extra hard about how she really felt. It was like she asked herself, 'At that time how did I really feel and what do I want my reader to feel when they read this?'

"You all seem to admire this ending because Lisa's feeling surprises us, but it also feels right. With all of that amazing swimming and diving, she probably *did* feel like a fish."

LINK

Remind children that they can revise their endings by adding strong feelings.

"So, guys, you have lots of choices you can make when you think about the work you want to do today as writers. You're so close to being ready to share your stories with the world! In addition to all of the other work you've been doing to revise your stories and get them ready to publish, you can practice reading your ending aloud and then revising the ending so it works even better. You might want to try adding in a strong feeling at the end, like Mem Fox did, or like Eric, or Lisa."

The rule of thumb is that in a good minilesson, we try to make one point. The truth is, however, that sometimes minilessons that make only a single point aren't worth their keep. You'll notice in this minilesson and in many others that I tuck in a few subordinate points. Here, I tuck in a bit of emphasis on reading our endings aloud well. I also mention what I notice when admiring the work of other authors (that the endings resolve the problem). This minilesson wouldn't work as well if I tried to give all these points equal weight.

Extending and Reinforcing Strategies for Strong Endings

AFTER TODAY'S MINILESSON, your kindergartners will head off to work on finishing their revised celebration piece. Usually your conferences and small-group work do not follow exclusively in the wake of your whole-class teaching. However, because today's lesson about endings happened at the end of the unit, and because endings are important, you may want to hold the same small group to teach strong endings over and over again. When it comes to learning something new, the sooner you can try that thing the more likely it will stick with you in the long run.

This group could start with you telling youngsters why you are working with them and what you hope to do in your time together. The beginning of my group might sound like this: "Remember how we were admiring the endings created by Eric and Lisa? What I want you to do right now is to reread the story you are going to publish and try to make a stronger ending for it."

I waited for a moment as each child read what he or she had already written. I reminded them to try reading their last line or last page with an ending voice, going down on the last words, so that they could *hear* if they had a powerful ending.

Then, I began. I want you to try doing what Eric and Lisa did. Ask yourself what you were really feeling at the end of that true time in your life. Then try writing an ending with true feelings."

As they all bent over their writing to give this work a try, I got prepared to notice as much as I could. Some children immediately started to write something, and other children went back to reread again. And some children were just sitting there. I decided to give feedback to the ones who had written something first. They were the easiest because they were showing me, what they already understood about endings. And, I was hoping that my coaching of these kids would help the other two subgroups.

I quickly read the endings of the two writers who had produced an ending. They both had a feeling there that worked. So I first showed their work to the other writers, nudging them on. Then I decided to extend the work the first two children had done.

I said, "You guys did end your story with a feeling. So now I am wondering if I can get you to think a little more about endings? At the end of Eric's story, he is frustrated, but he doesn't write, 'I was frustrated.' Instead, he shows that by writing what he said or did or thought. 'Pat, pat, pat. . . .' he writes. I think you two are ready to do the same. Think about how you acted or what you said, and try that as your ending. "Would you guys try now to end with a feeling? Just give it a go. When you are done with your try at a new ending, you can go back to your other work."

MID-WORKSHOP TEACHING   Your Work is Never Done

"Hey, everyone. I see some people who have done some work on their piece for our celebration, and now they are just sitting in their seats, not really doing anything. Remember that writing work is never over until our workshop time runs out. If you can't think of something else to do with your story for the celebration right now, you could go to some other stories in your folder and make them a little better, too. Any practice you do using your new learning will help you carry these tools with you as we move from this unit to the next one."

Using More Precise Language to Describe Emotions

Teach students about shades of different feelings by showing them a visual chart.

As soon as all of my kindergarten writers had returned to the rug, I said, "I saw so many of you trying to end your stories like Eric or Lisa. You were writing, 'I was happy,' or 'I was sad,' or 'I was mad.' So many of you were thinking about revising your endings in this new way.

"Well, happy can have more shades to it. You know how, in a really amazing box of crayons, there are several shades of a color? Like there is fuchsia red and red raspberry and fire engine red and red-orange. Well, when it comes to feelings, like happy, there are shades of happy."

I said, "If you are a little happy, someone might say you are glad, and if you are even more happy, you might be delighted. And, if you are even more happy than that, you might say you are thrilled. The same is true for being sad. If you are over the top sad, you could say you are miserable. If you're sort of in the middle sad, you are probably upset, and a little sad, you may just be blue.

"I want you to remember a time when you were angry about something. Make the face that matches how you felt." Lilly twisted her face at me, and I said, "Oh, Lilly, you look furious. And, Aiden, you look a little less angry, so maybe you are grumpy.

"So you see? Writers pay attention to and include feelings in their writing. Today we learned that there are shades of feelings. Now, when you are writing feelings into your stories, try to put in the exact shade of happy or sad or angry."

Writers Make Their Pieces Beautiful to Get Ready for Publication

IN THIS SESSION, you'll teach students how to make a piece beautiful in service to adding depth to their story.

GETTING READY

✔ Students will have already chosen the pieces they plan to publish and share; have students come to the rug with them, or have the stories ready to pass out while students are in the class meeting area (see Active Engagement)

✔ Class story (see Teaching)

✔ Containers of crayons and/or colored pencils ready to pass out to students (see Active Engagement)

T HIS SESSION IS A PERENNIAL FAVORITE among kindergartners because it is very celebratory! What's not to love about spending time fancying up a story, adding color, and getting it ready to share? But this session is not just about coloring—instead, we encourage you and your students to think deeply about what it means to prepare a story to meet its audience, because that is really the root of what you are asking students to do here: to consider their audience, and to make their stories as appealing and alluring as possible, to draw their audience in.

I suggest providing students with several options as they prepare their pieces. In this case, adding color, adding any missing bits to their drawings, and fixing messy words. This unit has built-in opportunities throughout for students to focus on making their writing easier to read, including editing and revision. So focus this session mostly on the aesthetics of a piece to be shared, aesthetics that are in service of meaning!

If we don't say otherwise, many kindergartners' idea of what it means to make something beautiful involves excessive use of stars, hearts, rainbows, lightning bolts, and so on. You'll want to make sure that students' beautification is in service of adding depth to the actual story, not just adding unrelated decorations. So when you present the work of the day, firmly root it in the context of the students' stories. Read the words of your story, search your memories, and see what you can add that will make your story beautiful, yes, but also clearer and richer.

Students will be getting their pieces ready to share with "readers" in the abstract, but also they will literally be imagining certain individuals. Many students even plan to present their stories to someone in particular, as a gift. Kindergartners love to give presents almost as much as they like to receive them. What an amazing concept, right?! That *writing* could be a gift?! How wonderful to have a class full of people who give writing as a gift to the world. Harness your children's gift-giving energy and let it drive their work today.

COMMON CORE STATE STANDARDS: W.K.3, W.K.5, W.K.6, RFS.K.1, RFS.K.2, RFS.K.3, SL.K.1, SL.K.6, L.K.1, L.K.2

Writers Make Their Pieces Beautiful to Get Ready for Publication

CONNECTION

◆ COACHING

Remind students of all that they have learned during this unit of study and all that they will be celebrating.

"This is a really exciting and important day, everyone. You've worked so hard not only to capture true stories from your lives but also to make those stories easy for you and everyone else to read. But you haven't stopped there! You've also learned lots of ways to revise your true stories to make them better and better. You certainly have a lot to celebrate! But before you get ready to share your pieces with your friends and families, there's some really important work left to do."

This will probably be the drumroll to your students' second author celebration. That makes today a big occasion.

Using an analogy—in this case, cooking—describe how a beautiful presentation lures readers in.

"Did you know that chefs who work in fancy restaurants have a saying, 'You eat with your eyes first'?" A few giggles erupted and an incredulous, "With your *eyes*?!" from the back of the rug somewhere. I continued with a smile, "Well, not *actually* with your eyes, of course. What chefs mean when they say that is that when food *looks* really beautiful and delicious, people can't wait to dig in—the way the food looks is the first thing that lures them in. If you had to choose between a big pile of food all mixed together like a hodgepodge and a plate where everything was beautifully and carefully arranged, you'd probably go for the beautiful one, right?

"Well, it's just the same with your stories. When writers take time to make their stories beautiful, when they are super careful and thoughtful about making them look exactly right, readers just can't wait to dig in and start reading! You've done incredible work writing, drawing, making your stories easy to read, and revising until they are just the way you want them. Now your stories deserve to be made beautiful, so readers practically start drooling, they want to read them so badly!"

❖ **Name the teaching point.**

"Today I want to teach you that before writers share their stories with an audience, they spend time making sure their writing is as clear and beautiful as possible—just like chefs work hard to make a meal look as good as it tastes! Here are three ways you can do that: you can add missing bits to your drawings, you can add color to your pictures, and you can check your words to make sure they are not too messy to read."

TEACHING

Using the class text, ask students to think of specific ways to prepare it to be shared with an audience.

"Let's imagine that we're getting ready to share our class story about when I had poop on my shoe, with an audience—well, in fact, we are. We could totally share this piece with our visitors tomorrow, right? So, let's think about what we need to do to make this story *so* beautiful, readers will not be able to wait to dig in!

"First, let's reread the words of our story. Why don't we do it all together? We know this story really well by now, right? And as we read the words, also be looking around in your memory, thinking about which of these three things—adding missing bits to the pictures, adding color, or fixing up messy words—you might want to do to make our story beautiful and ready to share."

Gesturing for the students to join in and read with me the best they could, I began reading. (See Figure. 19–1.)

"So what do you think we should do? It does look pretty good already. But turn and talk to your partner about what you think would be good to add—is anything missing from the pictures? What places really need color? Do you see any messy words that could be fixed up?"

After children discussed for a moment, I refocused the class and said, "I heard Harry saying that he thinks we should color in our rug, so everyone can tell that this happened right here. Good idea. Harry, why don't you come up here and add that to this picture? I've got crayons and colored pencils up here for you to use. While Harry is working, what else do you think could be added to our story?"

"We need to change the faces of us in the story," said Antonia. "We need to look like we are going to vomit!" "Yeah," Gustavo cheered, "and maybe some speech bubbles, too! We could put stuff like *gross* and *disgusting* in the bubbles."

"Absolutely! Antonia, come on up. I have a big eraser here. You might need to erase our first try at drawing our faces and make them over again, matching them to our true feelings. Our class story is so big, I think you will both fit. Gustavo, you can go right after they are done.

We'd spent a couple of interactive writing sessions since the story's inception finishing it up, so you'll see the finished version below. Interactive writing is a great way to practice all of the skills students are learning during word study time and during writing workshop—and a great time to finish up class texts!

It was morning meeting. We were counting the days of school with straws. Suddenly, someone said, "What is that smell?"

Our teacher was sad to find poop on my shoe. We also saw poop on the rug. Poop was on the new rug. We all felt nauseous.

Our teacher said, "Everyone check your shoes!" We all checked the bottom of our shoes. Kids were calling, "It's not me. Nothing on my shoes."

FIG. 19–1

"Did you guys see how we were really looking closely at a story that we were sure was done, and when we did that close looking, we found several places where we could make this story even more appetizing?"

ACTIVE ENGAGEMENT

Channel students to try this work in the context of their own stories by asking them to find a place they'll make beautiful.

"Now it is your turn. You're going to each get started trying this out in your own stories, right here and now. I've got cans of crayons and colored pencils up here that I'm borrowing from our art center, and in a second I'm going to put them around the rug so that you can all reach some. The crayons and colored pencils are new tools to add to our tool belt—they're just right for the fancying-up work we're doing now. Remember, as you take these new tools, that you are not just using them to do art! You are writers using these tools to tell more meaningful and more beautiful stories. So, before you just start going wild with these fun tools, make sure you take a second to think about what you will use them for.

Take a moment to reread the story you have decided to publish, and find one place that you want to add to or fix, right here on the rug. When you've found that place, put your finger on it and look up at me."

After the expected busy-ness of passing out the stories and settling the students into their work (and with a little pointed nudging from me, in some cases), they each pointed to a place in their stories and looked up.

Ask students to turn and tell their partners what they plan to do to fix up the part of their story they have chosen, and then to begin doing that work right then and there.

"Great, you're all ready—tell your partners what you're planning to work on. And then get started doing that, right now on the rug." As the students talked and got started working, I voiced over some things I saw happening: "Wow, Rafi is coloring his new shoes black in this picture in his story about getting new shoes with his dad. Now I know right away what color they were! Beautiful! Susanna is adding the knobs on the stove—she forgot before—beautiful!"

LINK

Remind students of the ways that writers prepare stories to share with an audience and encourage them to try out each of them.

"Everyone, great work—your stories are already looking so beautiful and delicious, readers will want to dig right in! Keep this up as I send you back to your work spots. Table monitors, please grab a can of crayons and one of colored pencils as you go. And remember your work today—writers always spend time making their writing beautiful and appealing as they get it ready to share. You can add missing bits to your pictures, add color, or fix up messy words. Make sure you try out each of these three things today as you work. I can't wait to watch this all happen!"

Nudging Students to Finish

I T'S LIKELY THAT EVEN AT THIS LATE DATE, you will have some students who are still scrambling to finish up their pieces to publish. It can be helpful, as you approach the deadline of this unit, to keep a specific record just for keeping track of which writers are in which part of the writing process. This can be as simple as a page with a blank box for each child, and you can write in the gist of their story and what work they have left to do.

With this deadline-work recording sheet, I can call out to kids in the room little reminders about the work they still have left to do. This is a very different kind of work that I am doing because at this point in the unit, I am trying to teach the kids how to finish a project. With so much of the teaching in the unit being about the writing *process*, this is the time in the unit where I can help the kids obsess about making a beautiful *product*, too.

Depending on how many children are in the I-still-have-a lot-to-do boat, you'll want to make sure to circle up with them, either in a small group or in individual conferences. It may be that you pull together a group of kids who are struggling to finish. They may even be struggling in different ways, for different reasons. This is often the

MID-WORKSHOP TEACHING   **Transforming Stories into Great Gifts!**

"Writers, look up at me for a moment. William just said something so smart! He's going to give his story about eating pizza with his cousin Stevie *to his cousin*. William said, 'I'm going to color everything just like it was, so Stevie remembers it. He was wearing his Giants shirt that day. It's blue, see?' So smart.

"Stories are the best gifts ever. It's such a great idea to think about who you might want to give your story to as a gift. And listen, everyone—when you are getting ready to give your story to someone as a gift, it's all the more reason to make it beautiful, with that person in mind. Stevie's going to love seeing that picture of him in his blue Giants shirt!"

As Students Continue Working . . .

"Writers, Juliser just found a place where she thought the words were not looking as beautiful as they could, so she taped some paper over that part and wrote the words again. You can do that too if you have that problem. Thanks for the idea, Juliser. And, Kris did that same thing with her picture on one of the pages. Her picture was not helping to tell her story, so she taped a piece of paper over her first try and tried again to make a meaningful picture. You can see how she used our drawing tips to help her make this a more beautiful, more meaningful page."

"Remember, writers, the color you're adding to your pictures needs to teach readers more about your story—you're not just coloring any old thing, you're adding color that shows more about what happened in your story!"

"Guys, Sam just asked me if it was too late to revise. He found a place that he wanted to add more details. Of course not! If you find a place that you want to revise and make even better, go ahead! It's never too late to revise."

case—one child may struggle because he keeps crossing out things and trying to make them "perfect," while another may struggle because she is still developing phonemic awareness, and it is still slow, laborious work getting letters for words on the page, while yet another may struggle because she has a hard time staying in her seat during writing time.

It's perfectly okay—and efficient, even—to call together a group of students and then to basically confer with them individually. You may do quick check-ins around the group and say something like, "I've noticed that you four are still working on finishing your stories, so you're not ready yet to add color to make them say even more. Let's check in about what's getting in the way."

After this quick informal assessment, you may choose to run a more traditional small group, in which you teach each student the same thing. Or, if they all need wildly different kinds of encouragement, you might just flit around the circle, like a butterfly with a lot of flowers to pollinate, giving mini-conferences tailored to each student's needs. You might want to keep them on the rug to work—sometimes a change of scenery and being in the company of others who are working on the same things can bring about the focus needed to finish up.

As those students are getting going, you'll of course want to circulate and make sure the rest of the class is on task as well—it can be big news to use crayons and colored pencils during writing workshop. Don't be surprised if, even though you've said it a jillion times, you find someone happily embellishing his story about the zoo with lightning bolts and the cool new cartoon dog his brother just taught him how to draw. You'll want to help children remind each other, as well, that the color they are adding is meaningful color, just as other elements of the drawings, and the words, are meaningful additions to the story.

Reading Our Writing Out Loud in Partnerships

Before sharing with an audience, writers practice reading their stories with a partner to build fluency.

"*Wow*, everyone. I've been cruising around admiring all of your work, and I have to tell you, if your stories were food, I would gobble them up! You've made them so beautiful, I think you're going to make your guests start drooling, they'll be so excited to read them. So . . . they *look* good. Another thing writers do to get ready to share their stories is to make sure they *sound* good.

"We worked a tiny bit on reading our stories a few days ago when we were learning about how to be great writing partners. Remember my reading of Maya's ladybug story?

"Since you're going to be reading your stories out loud to your visitors tomorrow, you're going to need to spend some time now practicing reading them to your partners so that when you read your writing, it sounds smooth and like a story. Turn so that you're facing your partner, and take turns reading to each other. Remember that you want your reading to sound smooth like a story, not like a robot! Remember, too, that you are reading your stories, treasuring each word as if it were gold!"

If there is time, you might even have your writers turn to face another partner and have them read their story again. Repeated reading is one of the most basic and most successful methods for improving fluency! Fluent, accurate, and easy reading will make visitors want to listen to their stories, and then hear about their work, during the celebration.

I crawled among my kindergarten students, coaching their reading. "Think about which parts should be read faster and which parts should be read more slowly. Try that page again," I called. Or, "That was your ending. Can you let me know that with your voice? Maybe make your voice go down quiet a little."

In that moment, even though the outside of me was all about the business of teaching writing, inside I was in awe. Their writing was awesome! That was the business of my inside as I crawled among my kindergarten writers.

Session 20

A Final Celebration
Bringing True Stories to Life

ear Teachers,

This unit is a hugely important one in your students' writing lives and is worth pulling out all of the stops to celebrate. Your students will have made monumental progress over the past several weeks, both in terms of capturing the sweet, poignant, and hilarious true stories from their own lives on paper, and in terms of beginning to internalize some of the conventions that make those stories readable. There are so many ways to celebrate—and of course you and your students will be brimming with your own ideas. The work I describe here is more than one session's worth, but I want to describe several options.

First I'll describe how you might celebrate students' work leading up to the actual celebration day by co-creating a bulletin board that highlights all of the new learning students have done in this unit of study. Then I'll describe an actual celebration day in which you turn your classroom into a museum where each child will share her work. You will, of course, pick and choose what makes sense for your classroom.

MINILESSON

As you begin, you'll want to remind the children about the growth you've seen across the unit and ask if they are willing to teach others what they've learned. You might say something like, "Writers, think back to the very first day of this unit, when we started talking about making our writing easy to read. Do you remember when you made two piles of writing, one that you could read easily and one that was tricky to read? Well, just think how huge your 'Easy to Read' pile is now! And that's not all—you've grown into writers who can capture the amazing true stories from your lives in writing. You all have given a lot of loving care to your writing. It has grown strong and detailed and lovely and long because you've revised it and thought hard about how to make it easy to read. Now it's time to celebrate the work you've done. As part of our celebration, I was thinking that maybe you'd be willing to teach other people what you've learned about writing and revising true stories that are easy to read. Would you be willing to do that?"

COMMON CORE STATE STANDARDS: W.K.3, W.K.6, RFS.K.1, RFS.K.2, RFS.K.3, SL.K.1, SL.K.4, SL.K.6, L.K.6

Of course they will be!

You might suggest that the class create a bulletin board to share the work of the unit, with each student annotating pieces other than the one they are planning to share in order to draw viewers' attention to specific things they've learned. As you explain that children will be reviewing their own stories and putting Post-it note flags in the places where they want readers to know what they've learned, you'll want to have the unit's charts on hand for reference.

You might say something like, "I was thinking that maybe, because you guys worked so hard on all of your pieces, we could take some of the other pieces from your folders and put them on our huge bulletin board in the hall. But instead of just hanging them there, you guys can decide what the important things you've learned are that you want people to pay attention to, and mark them with a little flag! We've done so much during this unit—we've talked about writing true stories that sound like you, we've talked about ways to make your writing easier to read, and you've helped each other do some wonderful revision work as well, to make your stories even better."

Narrative Writing Checklist

	Kindergarten	NOT YET	STARTING TO	YES!	Grade 1	NOT YET	STARTING TO	YES!
	Structure				**Structure**			
Overall	I told, drew, and wrote a whole story.	☐	☐	☐	I wrote about when I did something.	☐	☐	☐
Lead	I had a page that showed what happened first.	☐	☐	☐	I tried to make a beginning for my story.	☐	☐	☐
Transitions	I put my pages in order.	☐	☐	☐	I put my pages in order. I used words such as *and* and *then, so*.	☐	☐	☐
Ending	I had a page that showed what happened last in my story.	☐	☐	☐	I found a way to end my story.	☐	☐	☐
Organization	My story had a page for the beginning, a page for the middle, and a page for the end.	☐	☐	☐	I wrote my story across three or more pages.	☐	☐	☐
	Development				**Development**			
Elaboration	My story indicated who was there, what they did, and how the characters felt.	☐	☐	☐	I put the picture from my mind onto the page. I had details in pictures and words.	☐	☐	☐
Craft	I drew and wrote some details about what happened.	☐	☐	☐	I used labels and words to give details.	☐	☐	☐
	Language Conventions				**Language Conventions**			
Spelling	I could read my writing.	☐	☐	☐	I used all I knew about words and chunks of words (*at, op, it*, etc.) to help me spell.	☐	☐	☐
	I wrote a letter for the sounds I heard.	☐	☐	☐	I spelled all the word wall words right and used the word wall to help me spell other words.	☐	☐	☐
	I used the word wall to help me spell.	☐	☐	☐		☐	☐	☐

You'll explain to your students that you want them to pick three stories from their folders that show them trying different strategies to make those pieces better. Explain that after they each pick three stories, you'll be thinking together about what kinds of important things students learned during this unit that they might want to flag with a Post-it. This is a great time to draw their attention to the charts as well. You may even want to reread them together as a class.

Give your students a few minutes to read their stories to themselves, paying attention to places where they tried something new, something they want to share with readers—this could be something that makes their writing easier to read or it could be a revision strategy. You could ask students to put their fingers on one place they want to share their learning with readers and to turn and talk to a partner about it. It's helpful to have students share out some of these ideas as well, to help get everyone's juices flowing.

Explain to your students that you will be sending them off to their seats with three or four Post-it note flags each. Their work will be to reread their stories carefully, placing flags in places that they want to share something specific that they learned. You may ask students to write a little note to their readers on the sticky note, explaining what they did.

Some teachers prefer to divide up the class into smaller groups, with each group searching for and flagging a different element of their learning. For example, three students might be looking for and flagging a page that shows a time they added dialogue as a revision strategy. Three others might be searching for a page where they made sure to use a vowel in every word. If you choose to organize this way, you might say something like this before sending students off: "In your group, look first through your own writing, and then, if you need more examples, look through other kids' writing. Look for places where you did whatever your group is looking for. Use Post-it note tags to mark all the examples you find, and then reread them together!"

CONFERRING AND SMALL-GROUP WORK
Celebrating Growth and Noting Areas for Future Teaching

Your conferring work today is likely to involve providing some basic support to your students as they do this sophisticated evaluative work. You'll be circulating throughout the class, reminding students about all of the different kinds of work the unit has inspired, encouraging partnerships to help each other—in general, noticing and making a big deal about all that your students now know how to do. This work is not just about the bulletin board, of course. The bulletin board is a wonderful way to share specifics of your students' growth, but it also provides an opportunity for your students to reflect on and evaluate their own work. As you circulate today, you'll want to celebrate both what they have done and the fact that they are able to notice and discuss what they've done. You will also not be able to help noticing what each child still needs to learn how to do. Even though you will probably not be talking to the kids at this moment about their needs as writers, you will probably be dreaming of ways to carry those needs forward into your next unit of study.

Because you'll be busy getting ready for your celebration, you may choose to use your mid-workshop teaching time and teaching share time as more work time/conferring time so that students are as ready as they can be before the end of today's workshop. If you do choose to have a mid-workshop teaching point, you might just draw the class's attention to a partnership that is working well together—staying on task, supporting each other, noticing all that their partners have learned.

SHARE

The creation of your bulletin board is really your way to declare to the wider world what your children have learned during this unit. You might make your share about imagining what that bulletin board should look like. This is sort of a sneaky way to do a little non-narrative work at the end of your narrative unit. And, because your next unit will probably be an information writing unit, this share could provide a little warm-up for the dramatic shift in genre.

You might consider holding this share in the hallway. The children could all bring their marked-up stories out into the hall and have a seat facing the blank bulletin board. Then, you could lead the kids through the creation of a bulletin board. Your children have probably never put very much thought into the purpose of bulletin boards. You might begin by teaching your writers that bulletin boards teach the world what they have learned. To do this teaching, the board needs a title that talks about all of the parts. You can write the title on a sentence strip. Then the different parts of the board need a name so that people will know how the learning is organized. Again, you can record their heading ideas on sentence strips. And finally, your kindergartners can think about how they might display their pieces so that they serve as examples of each of the headings.

Involving your very young students in the process of creating a bulletin board can help make them more active learners. Who knows, maybe they will become the kind of learners that walk through the school trying to learn from (or doing critiques of) all the other bulletin boards. You could then use bulletin boards as a nonfiction text and show your kindergarten readers how to read to learn from those displays.

THE CELEBRATION: SETTING UP A TRUE STORIES MUSEUM

Young children keep us in touch with the need for celebration. Because we are teachers, there's not much chance that Valentine's Day or Halloween will slip by us unnoticed. How lucky we are to be in a profession that reminds us that life is richer when it is punctuated by a sense of occasion!

One way to keep the energy high is to vary our celebrations. In Natalie's classroom, we decided to invite parents, administrators, and older students and to turn the school library into a true stories museum. Each child was given his or her own "booth," and the child found a way to display work in progress that showed what he or she had done. To draw observers' attention to places where the children had made especially key revisions or worked particularly hard to make their stories easy to read, these young authors put little "Ask Me" Post-it note tags at particular places throughout their texts. The most efficient way to handle paper management is simply to have students use the pieces they have prepared for the bulletin board and to hang them (or copies of them) after the celebration is finished.

The day before our museum opened the children gave out invitations and practiced explaining their work during a dry run with writing partners (and, for some children, with Natalie and me). This preparation added to their excitement. We also assigned each child a spot—a "booth"—in which they would display and present their work to guests.

Before the visitors enter the "museum," it's important to explain the procedures to them. To help keep things running smoothly, we gave each visitor a list of the children they were to visit (in order). The last child on each visitor's list was that visitor's own child. We explained that we'd sound a bell every so often to let people know they only had two more minutes and would then need to move to the next child. We asked each visitor to fill in each child's response sheet, writing one very specific thing they admired that the child had done. The children were already waiting by their "booths," ready to present their work. It's important to stay on top of sounding the bell or whatever signal you've devised to keep things moving along. You can expect to set aside about forty minutes for this part of the celebration, give or take, depending on your class size and the number of guests.

When guests have made their way through their lists, gather everyone for a toast to the writers. Be sure to teach as you always do with demonstration and with explanation of purpose, even when what you are teaching is how to celebrate with a toast. In my celebration, after filling some Dixie cups with apple juice, I called for the attention of both the children and the adults.

"Everyone, I just want to thank you all for coming to help celebrate the amazing work of these writers during this unit of study. In order to celebrate, I thought we might toast. In our first celebration we also toasted to our success. However, because this time all of you have joined us and because toasting is a tradition in many different parts of the world, we thought we might toast again. Toasting is a way to honor something that is worthy of respect and admiration."

Looking at only my kindergarten students now, I continued. "You are all worthy of my respect and admiration. You have each worked so hard and grown so much during these weeks. Your stories are proof of that growth. So, I will begin the toasting by saying something nice, something true, and when I am done, you will raise your glass and declare, 'Hear, hear!' Then take a tiny sip of your apple juice because, if more people want to make a toast, you will need more juice left in your cup."

I offered up my toast, which sounded very much like what I had already said while explaining toasting to my kids. First one parent and then another said some very sweet things about the work these kids had done to make and tell beautiful true stories from their lives. And then, Malachi stood up.

He was one of my most eloquent students. He was also one of my most struggling writers. Malachi held his glass in the air very seriously and said, "All of you worked so hard to make it all clear. You did all kinds of things to make sure your writing was really clear for your readers. It was hard work, but it was fun, too!"

Raising his glass even higher, he said, "Congratulations, everyone!"

"Hear, hear," all of the voices called.

"Hear, hear," I thought.

Hear.

Here . . .

Lucy and Natalie

Jalen rides in the park.

I did a slam dunk. I spinned around. I felt like I was flying.

I did a slam dunk. I spinned around and dunk it. The other team was losing.

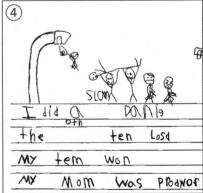

I did a slam dunk. The other team lost. My team won. My mom was proud of me.

FIG. 20–1 Jalen's basketball piece